Holiday Walks in the Alpujarra

Jeremy Rabjohns

Published by Sigma Leisure – an imprint of
Sigma Press, 1 South Oak Lane, Wilmslow, Cheshire SK9 6AR, England.

British Library Cataloguing in Publication Data
A CIP record for this book is available from the British Library.

ISBN: 1-85058-786-8

Typesetting and Design by: Sigma Press, Wilmslow, Cheshire.

Cover design by: Sigma Press

Printed by: Ashford Colour Press Ltd

Cover illustration and line drawings: cover from a pastel painting by Jeni Rabjohns; pen and ink line drawings by Jeni Rabjohns.

Maps: the author

DISCLAIMER

Preface

One of the joys of being both a guide and a resident of the Alpujarra is that of introducing people to the area, and meanwhile seeing it afresh through their eyes. Through these pages I hope to show many more of you the joy of being here and to demonstrate what captivated us. I have tried to make the book your 'local friend' and through it, to share my experience of The Alpujarra, giving you what I hope will be an instant but deep appreciation.

By visiting the villages described, walking around as much as you are able and using the guide to the full, you will gain more experience than many residents have. Certainly in a physical sense you will, since many native-born residents of the area have barely left their home village throughout their entire lives; I think it's because they are happy there and see no reason to go elsewhere.

The routes described are circular and have start points accessible by car, the vast majority also by public bus. There is enough information in the appendices to enable you to plan your own multi-centre holiday or use one of the holiday companies listed that provide packages or tailor-made holidays.

I do not attempt to cover in any detail the peaks of the Sierra Nevada. In that terrain the landscape defies the writing of detailed descriptive notes and walkers should only be there if confident of their own navigational skills. In three walks I have been tempted to the peaks. These could be used as access routes by the experienced hill walkers and mountaineers amongst you who wish to make expeditions to the many 3000m peaks of the Sierra Nevada. The rest of us will have a bath, put our feet up and think of you in your freezing bivvy.

Every care has been taken to be accurate in description and mapping but, if a bomb had dropped on your walk, I offer my abject apologies in advance. The background notes and musings of a rambling author are intentionally of a personal nature but I am sure they will add to most people's appreciation of the walks. If you would prefer me to shut up and get on with the walk, you will soon learn that the notes are visually separated from the step by step description and so can be easily ignored.

Finally may I wish you a stress-free holiday and presume to welcome you on behalf of The Alpujarreños, asking you, by the way, to be tolerant of our strange ways. We, in turn, will not complain about your coffee and will go to bed quietly at 10.30pm when we visit you.

Jeremy

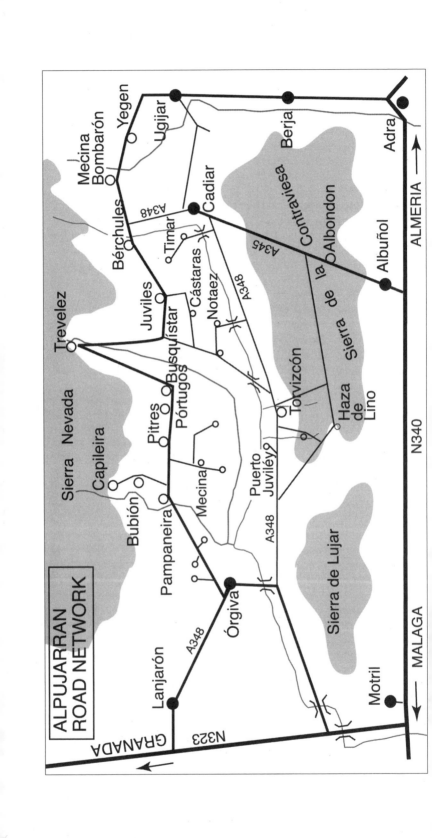

Contents

Free Internet Update Service

This book will be updated whenever it is reprinted, but be sure to check our website for updates and corrections in the meantime. This service is completely free of charge – just go to the "updates" section on our web site at: **www.sigmapress.co.uk**

We welcome your input to this service – if you encounter any problems on the walks or have any comments, please send your suggestions to us either by post (address on back cover) or by e-mail to: **info@sigmapress.co.uk**

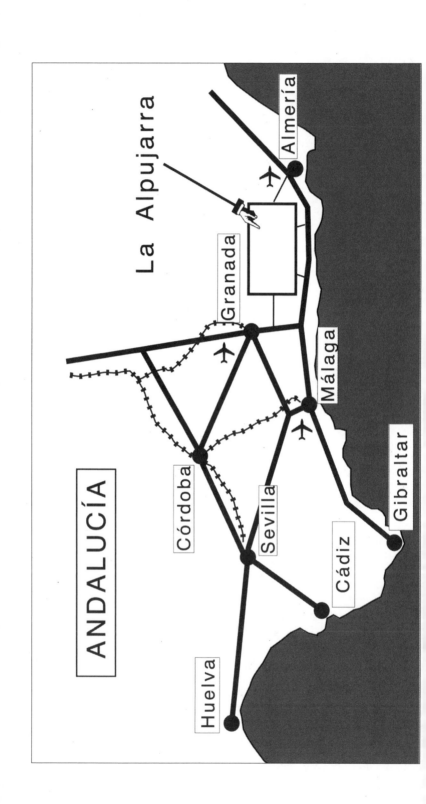

Introducing The Alpujarra

Using this guidebook

To help plan a holiday, sections are given below on travel and accommodation. Appendix D lists some contacts who either offer services or complete packages. Whether travelling by car or public transport enough information is given to enable any of the locations mentioned in the text to be reached. The bus timetables given in Appendix A, although liable to change, have not altered over the past seven years.

The walks are separated into chapters based on individual villages, or in one case a group of villages in the same valley, where the traveller may find himself staying or passing through. Arbitrarily, these chapters are in a sequential west to east order. A car driver might do well to base himself centrally and spread out in either direction while a user of the buses would do better to start at one end and progress. In either case, a visit to Pampaneira and its information and exhibition centre is well worth while early in the itinerary to get an appreciation of the area and stock up on leaflets, books and maps.

The sketch maps give enough information to enable the walks to be followed. The descriptive **Notes** provide a backup, but it should not be necessary to follow every dot and comma slavishly. One of the topographical maps suggested in the 'kit list' below should always be carried to give an overall picture and to cover the possibility of wandering off the area covered by the sketch map. The maps vary in scale, but each has a grid showing kilometre squares giving an at-a-glance indication of scale. The grid is orientated to the page and bears no relation to any standard mapping grid system. Arrows on the maps show the direction of the walk along the various features such as road, path or river and each map has numbers along the route which cross-refer to the descriptive **Notes**.

Each walk also has a profile diagram (Appendix E) showing its length in kilometres and the amount of ascent and descent in metres. These are all reproduced to the same scale and so, once a walk has been done, they will give a good guide as to the relative effort required and time to be taken by future walks.

At the beginning of the **Notes** for each walk a probable duration is given. This is subjective, but the times given are real ones that have been experienced by your middle-aged author and his companions. We have a tendency to sit, stare, eat and drink rather a lot so in all probability the timings are overestimates. So much depends on weather, season and mood but in the absence of other information the times will give a good indication. Also, at the beginning of the **Notes** any necessary warnings are given.

Scattered through the **Notes** are sections of background information which are visually distinct and can be ignored for route finding but which hopefully, will add to your appreciation of the walks.

Kit list

The 1:25,000 IGN maps provide a good topographical background to accompany the sketch maps in this guide, but don't trust them as regards the paths and tracks marked (or not marked). The sheets required to cover the walks described are 1028 I, 1028 III, 1027 IV, 1042 I, II, III, IV, 1043 I, 1056 II. Two other map/guides cover most of the area in one sheet, at 1:40000 (ISBN 84-8090-075-1) and at 1:50000 (ISBN 84-931217-1-1). Available from The Map Shop 01684 593146, www.themapshop.co.uk.

A wide range of temperatures can be experienced at any time of year. If visiting The Alpujarra with a view to the walking you should avoid high summer. From June to September, 35°C shade temperatures are normal; walking in the afternoon sun during this period is no fun and quite dangerous. If specifically aiming for the peaks of the Sierra Nevada, summer is a good time since there is little snow and the temperatures at higher altitudes are tolerable. Light clothing with long sleeves and trousers protect the skin and help prevent dehydration but warm and waterproof layers need to be carried at these higher altitudes.

Spring, autumn and winter walking is a pleasure but you need to be prepared for hot days and cold nights. For much of the year it is worth having some gloves and a woolly hat in the rucksack as well as sun hat, shorts and sun cream. For the higher more remote walks you should be equipped with some form of survival bag, compass, emergency food, whistle and know what you are expected to do with them.

Dogs are numerous, noisy and cowardly, but if you are nervous of them, then it might be worthwhile investing in a 'dog dazer' to give confidence. An anti-histamine cream in the first aid kit is a good idea to alleviate any plant or insect stings.

In the same way that we now have walking poles instead of sticks we have drinking systems instead of a bottle. A good idea since, with a mouth-piece always at the ready, a frequent intake is more likely than when the bottle is at the bottom of the rucksack. Dehydration and heat exhaustion are as life-threatening as hypothermia.

Travelling to The Alpujarra

The Alpujarra is in the Province of Granada in Andalucia, the southernmost autonomous region of Spain. Road access is good, and in two days one can arrive by road from any part of Spain. Granada city is on the railway route from Madrid. Three airports are used to varying extents:

Málaga

The most common choice. Used by charter companies and airlines providing direct flights from all major UK regional airports. Málaga is at least 2½ hours by car from The Alpujarra and at least 4½ hours by public bus.

Almería

Another good choice, particularly if aiming at the eastern end of The Alpujarra. Flights are less frequent and the choice of airports more restricted. Thursdays and/or Sundays from Manchester, Birmingham or Gatwick depending on season. Transfer times to The Alpujarra by car from Almería are 1¾ hours and 3½ hours by public bus.

Granada

Is the nearest airport to the area, about 1½ hours by car. There are currently no direct flights from the UK. Iberia have scheduled services to Granada from London but changing at Madrid.

Car Hire

Booked at the same time as booking a flight is just as economic as hiring at the airport. Hiring a car for two weeks costs the same as a return taxi fare from Malaga to Alpujarra.

Public Buses

They are comfortable, reliable and cheap but obviously tend to make journey times slower and less convenient. Time-tables have never varied over the years – see Appendix A.

Travel within the area

A lot depends on whether a fixed or multi-centre holiday is planned. If planning to move on from place to place this can be done quite easily using the buses. The exception to this is between the villages of Bérchules and Mecina Bombarón which have no direct bus link. A car is much more useful in a fixed centre situation.

   Taxis exist but are are not easily found. The list of telephone numbers of known taxis is given with the bus timetables in the Appendix A. Where they are easily found this is mentioned in the fact file under the chapter headings.

Local lingo

Below is a list of village names and pronunciations to help with asking the way or buying tickets. Stressed syllables are underlined and have an acute accent.

Atalbéitar	[Atal-bay-ee-tar]
Bérchules	[Bear-chew-les]
Bubión	[Booby-on]
Busquístar	[Bus-kissed-ah]
Capileira	[Kapil-eh-ee-ra]
Cástaras	[Kast-aras]
Ferreirola	[Ferr-e-ee-roller]
Fondales	[Fon-dhal-ez]

Haza de Lino	[<u>Ath</u>-a del <u>Lee</u>-no]
Juviles	[Who-<u>bill</u>-ez]
Mecina	[Meth-<u>een</u>-a]
Mecinilla	[Meth-in-<u>ee</u>-yah]
Mecina Bombarón	[Meth-<u>een</u>-a Bomba-<u>ron</u>]
Notaez	[No-<u>tie</u>-eth]
Órgiva	[<u>Ore</u>-hiba]
Pampaneira	[Pampan-eh-<u>ee</u>-ra]
Pitres	[<u>Pea</u>-tres]
Pórtugos	[<u>Poor</u>-too-gos]
Puerto Juviléy	[Pooh-<u>air</u>-tow Who-bill-<u>lay</u>]
Tímar	[<u>Tea</u>-mar]
Torvizcón	[Torvith-<u>kon</u>]
Ugíjar	[Oo-<u>he</u>-ha]
Yegen	[<u>Yeh</u>-hen]

Accommodation

Nearly every village has rooms of some sort available. *Pensión*, or *hostal*, are the most common, they have a star system which doesn't mean much in practice. Usually the facilities are better than those suggested by their rating. Equally, hotels are not necessarily any better or more expensive than *hostal*.

Prices quoted are per room so, assuming two people sharing, the bill is always a pleasant surprise when judged by UK standards. Apart from the above, signs advertising *fonda*, *posada*, *habitaciones* and *camas* are also seen and these are guest houses of various standards.

Self-catering accommodation is also relatively easy to find on the spur of the moment or in advance using one of the agenceies listed in Appendix D. The magic words to look for are *'se alquila'*, *'casa'*, *'apartamentos'*, and *'alojamientos rurales'*.

There is usually no problem of bed shortage but; there are certain times of the year when booking ahead is definitely advisable. Christmas and New Year, Easter and August are particularly busy with Spanish visitors and individual villages have their special *fiesta* periods when they are full to the last shared bunk bed. See list of suggested lodgings, Appendix B.

Food and Drink

An adventurous walker should be adventurous with his food. Eating out in The Alpujarra is cheap so there are no worries there; it doesn't really matter if you don't understand the menu, just order a few dishes and enjoy what comes. Having seen a few menus with English translations I know they are quite creative and need taking with a pinch of salt. Having said all that, I relent and refer you to the glossary of dishes below which covers most of the common dishes.

There is a big problem for vegetarians; the concept is little understood. "You don't eat meat?"

"No."

"Well, have some ham instead."

"No thank you, I don't eat meat."

"OK. Here, have this fish."

"No thank you, I don't eat meat."

"Oh, so you don't eat meat. Why are you alive?"

"I don't know, I just eat vegetables, dairy produce and eggs, could I have a plate of beans please?"

"Certainly, here you are. I've put some black pudding with them for the flavour."

"Thank you!"

The committed vegetarian has to be very careful, hungry or egg-bound. Pitres has a restaurant (El Jardin), devoted to international vegetarian food. 'Ibero Fusion' of Capileira also has vegetarian dishes.

The Alpujarra is slightly too far from the coast to have traditional fish cuisine but fresh fish does arrive daily. The traditional way of eating fish in the area is to use salt cod, *bacalao*. These are very good dishes; once the unappetising leathery slab of cod has been soaked for a day it transforms into surprisingly succulent cod with all the right flavour and texture.

A very hospitable custom of the Province of Granada is to give a *tapa* with any drink of beer or wine ordered. The *tapa* is not a right but will normally be given, depending on the bar and the time of day. A few drinks taken before a meal time and you will find out what the kitchen is made of. If you enjoyed your tapa then you can order a full portion, *una ración*. It is often the case that the more up market the establishment the poorer the *tapa*.

Unless you are in a formal up-market restaurant situation the best way to eat is to choose a selection of *raciónes*, three would be enough to feed two people, and share what comes. You may not be given plates individually, the customary way to eat being to eat from a common dish picking with your fork.

Menu del dia is an alternative to *raciónes* if you want a three-course meal at midday with minimal cost. You will be given a choice of two or three dishes for each course.

A custom observed even in up-market restaurants that surprises many visitors, is that of retaining your knife and fork for all the courses. You normally remove them from the plate when you have finished, making life easy for the waiter, and washer-upper.

The wines offered are always Spanish. The locally produced wine, *vino costa*, is a rosé often ageing to brown. It is not fortified but has a sherry-like flavour and strength. Worth a try, but an aquired taste;

they vary a lot so don't give up after the first try. Local producers are starting to bottle white and red wines and if you want to try these you should ask for *vino blanco de terreno* or *vino tinto de terreno*.

Breakfast in Spain is not normally the first thing you do with your day. Having eaten late the night before, most people go about their business for an hour or two before stopping for breakfast. This is why it seems that whoever you want to find in the morning, from the bank manager to the taxi driver, they have all "Just popped out. Call back later."

Breakfast is usually a *tostada*. You will be offered a variety of toppings, (see glossary of foods below); why not take advantage of the abundant olive oil and try simply the oil or my favourite, a pulverised mixture of fresh tomato and garlic. To go with the coffee there's no harm in a small brandy, except that you are never given a small one. Share it with a friend. Many people drink a mixture of brandy and sweet anis for breakfast. This goes down very easily, ask for *sol y sombra* [sol ee <u>som</u>-bra], literally "sun and shade", they will know what you mean.

A Glossary of Foods

(V) indicates vegetarian

aceite	[a-<u>thay</u>-itay]	oil (olive)
almendra	[al-<u>men</u>-dra]	almond
ajillo	[a-<u>he</u>-yo]	a garlic sauce for meat dishes
arroz	[a-<u>roth</u>]	rice. Used as a term for a paella-type dish.
arroz con leche	[~kon <u>lech</u>-e]	rice pudding. One of the four Spanish puddings! Served cold. Much nicer than it sounds.
bacalao	[back-al-<u>ow</u>]	cod. Usually salt cod but you should not be able to tell.
berenjenas fritas	[beren-<u>hen</u>-as <u>free</u>-tas] (V)	fried aubergine slices, very good.
bocadillo	[bokka-<u>dee</u>-yo]	sandwich of the baguette type
boquerónes	[bok-air-<u>ron</u>-ez]	anchovies, fresh, not those salty things in tins.
~*fritas*	[~<u>freet</u>-tas]	fresh deep-fried anchovy
~*en vinagre*	[~en bin-<u>nag</u>-ray]	soused anchovy
calamares	[kala-<u>ma</u>-rez]	squid, normally fried rings

6

cazuela	[kath-<u>well</u>-a]	casserole dish of almost anything
cazuela de arroz	[kath-<u>well</u>-a de a-<u>roth</u>]	especially good. Basically a soupy version of a meat paella
chipirónes	[chipi-<u>ron</u>-ez]	young bite-sized squid, fried or in sauce
chorizo	[cho-<u>rith</u>-oh]	spicy sausage, fried in chunks. Larger diameter *chorizo* is sold sliced ready for picnic use in the shops
choto	[<u>cho</u>-toe]	a casserole of kid, usually with potato and garlic
café con leche	[ka-<u>fay</u> kon <u>lech</u>-e]	white coffee
café cortado	[ka-<u>fay</u> kor-<u>tar</u>though]	white coffee with less milk
café manchado	[ka-<u>fay</u> man-<u>cha</u>-though]	white coffee with less coffee
café solo	[ka-<u>fay</u> <u>sol</u>-o]	black coffee
casero(a)	[kas-<u>air</u>-row]	home made
cerdo	[<u>thair</u>-dough]	pork
chuleta	[chew-<u>let</u>-a]	chop, fried or griddled, pork unless otherwise stated, with chips.
conejo	[kon-<u>e</u>-hoe]	rabbit, usually as a casserole
cordero	[kord-<u>air</u>-row]	lamb
ensalada	[ensal-<u>arth</u>-a]	green salad. Vegetarians beware of tuna often used as garnish.
flan	[flan]	the ubiquitous pudding, crème caramel. Get to like it or go without.
gachas	[<u>gach</u>-ass]	not often seen but a traditional dish cooked in homes. Try it in the restaurant *Artesa Bubión*. A sauce of some sort on top of a cooked dumpling mixture. Cooked on the plate.

7

habas con jamón	[<u>ab</u>-baz kon ham-<u>on</u>]	best in early spring or the broad beans will be frozen. A great dish trimmed with a little air-cured ham.
jamón	[Ham-<u>on</u>]	world-famous air-cured ham of The Alpujarra. You *will* try it!
lomo (a la plancha)	[<u>Lom</u>-oh]	(griddled) pork loin slices, previously marinated and usually served with chips. A good thing to ask for in a *bocadillo* to take-away.
longaniza	[Longan-<u>ee</u>-tha]	another spicy sausage
mantequilla	[mantech-<u>key</u>-ya]	butter
mermelada	[mare-meh-<u>lah</u>-tha]	jam – don't expect to find marmalade
migas	[<u>me</u>-gas]	Spanish version of cous-cous, can be served with anything but usually fried fish or peppers.
morcilla	[more-<u>thi</u>-ya]	blood pudding. Especially worth trying if you don't like black pudding
pan	[pan]	bread
~ *de higo*	[pan day <u>ee</u>-go]	a small slab of finely chopped dried figs with spices. Excellent.
patatas	[pat-<u>tat</u>-taz]	potatoes
papas	[<u>pap</u>-az]	potatoes
papas a lo pobre or *patatas a lo pobre (V)*	[pat-<u>tat</u>-taz a low <u>pob</u>-ray]	a royal potato dish for a poor man. Thinly sliced potato cooked slowly in olive oil with garlic, peppers, cumin. Usually served with a fried egg
plato alpujarreño	[<u>plat</u>-oh alpooh-ha-<u>ren</u>-yo]	all the pig you can eat in the form of ham and the various sausages. Comes with *patatas a lo pobre* and an egg. Share it with a friend or be a pig.

pollo	[po̲y-yo]	chicken, often chopped into unrecognisable joints and in a delicious *ajillo sauce*.
potaje	[pot-a̲-hay]	
puchero	[poo-chai̲r-row]	soups cum casseroles, always good, may contain pulses.
queso	[ke̲s-oh]	cheese – you ask for cheese, you get cheese, with no frills. Not a bad thing to ask for as a pudding given the shortage of puddings. It's usually goat's cheese or a mixture of goat, sheep and cow.
~ *de cabra*		(goat)
~ *de oveja*		(sheep)
~ *de almendra*		basically marzipan
queso con miel	[ke̲s-oh kon me-e̲l]	a young bland cheese drizzled with honey, rarely offered but a good sweet.
sopa	[so̲p-pa]	soup
~*de ajo*	[day a̲-hoe]	a great soup, thin but flavoursome with bread chunks in it.
~ *de picadillo*	[picka-de̲e-yo]	thin ham-flavoured soup with some noodles and chopped hard-boiled egg.
salchichón	[salchi-cho̲n]	my favourite spicy sausage, peppery, served cold and thin sliced like salami.
tortilla	[tor-te̲a-ya]	omelette
tortilla de patatas (V)		the Spanish omelette
tostada	[tossed-a̲r-tha]	toasted bread
~ *con aceite*		with olive oil
~ *con tomate*		with tomato and garlic
~ *con mantequilla*		with butter

Language

Don't expect to find any Spaniard in The Alpujarra who speaks English. The bigger hotels and the information centre have a basic knowledge but don't expect them to understand your gabbled tongue. The best plan is to at least learn a few words and essentially, their correct pronunciation.

Working through the first few lessons of a tape-based course for beginners will give enough language to make you feel confident in simple bar and shopping situations. It will also double the pleasure you get from your holiday by getting the Spaniards you meet on your side of the language barrier. A free, distance-learning course in Spanish is offered by Manchester Institute for Information Delivery (MiiD); Email: spanishonline@miid.net;
web site: www.miid.net/spanishonline.

On entering shops or bars, it is important to say something, a greeting to all and sundry, this seems to establish your existence and position in the queue. Chance meetings in the countryside also appear very ugly if no greeting is made. Try to learn enough to say something relevant about the weather or the pretty village. A "buenas dias" might break the ice but some follow-up comment perhaps complimenting the flowers or vegetable plot will be an occasion for the beaming smile to break out and you will be replied to incomprehensibly, then your beaming smile will break out and everybody will have gained. So much better than walking morosely past each other in silence. You will go home with a better impression of your hosts and you will leave a better impression of visitors. It is not easy to learn a language but it is far easier for you to learn one; than for your hosts to learn the dozen or so needed to deal with all their visitors.

A few words or phrases, that is all that's needed. Think what a big step forward it was when you or your child said their first words – what an advance on screaming.

A Bit of Background
Geology

The geology of the region is complex; to cover the subject fully would require treatises on continental drift, some very long words and big numbers. For we laymen it is a convenient escape to know that it is complex and we may be forgiven not fully understanding what we see. The southern part of Andalucia is, apparently, a little bit of Africa superimposed on Europe. Subsequent liftings and foldings have fragmented and mixed strata from distant sources and ages. The uplifting of the Sierra Nevada continues today and occasional weak earthquakes emphasise the continuing instability of the region.

The mountains that have been raised in this manner reach to almost 3,500m from sea-level in the space of 30km. Subsequent to their formation, ice ages had their effect in cutting the main valleys falling from the ridge of today. They were sub-divided by more recent lesser ice-ages and the *barrancos* that start their course above a height of 2500m are mostly of this origin. The most notable and easily appreciated glacial remains can be seen in the area known as "Las Siete Lagunas" which is visited by a walk described in the chapter "Trevelez".

The heights of the Sierra Nevada are in a bio-climatic zone not far short of tundra; ice deposits from previous geological periods have been found and are being studied. The Mediterranean coast of Spain has climates ranging from desert to semi-tropical and so by taking an imaginary walk from the mouth of the Río Guadalfeo to the source of one of its tributaries on Mulhacén one would potentially pass through all the bio-climatic zones of Europe from semi-tropical to tundra in the space of 50km. This variety of geology and climate makes The Alpujarra a joy to walk in. In the course of a week's walking, if not in a single walk, one sees much variety and those that like to stop, stare and appreciate during their walks will find many opportunities to regain their breath and perhaps to have it taken away again.

Flora and Fauna

With this range of climates it is not surprising to find a great variety of vegetation zones and habitats. The most conspicuous group of animals is, as everywhere, the insects and the main pleasure amongst these is to see a great number of butterflies almost all the year round.

Reptiles are numerous and those with an interest in them will find The Alpujarra a happy hunting ground. The terrapins found in the Río Guadalfeo, *(clemys caspica and Emys orbicularis)* being my favourite find. The adder *(vipera latasti)* is present at altitudes of about 1500m but is less commonly seen than in the UK. This is the only venomous snake. Amphibians are common and give serenades throughout spring and summer nights.

Most of the birds present are also known in the UK; some notable and spectacular exceptions commonly seen are the hoopoe *(upupa epops)*, golden oriole *(oriolus oriolus)* and the bee-eater *(merops apiastre)*. It is a joy to see and hear others that are as common as muck like the nightingale *(luscinia megarhynchas)* and turtle dove *(streptopelia turtur)*. Ornithologists will find plenty to interest them amongst the less obvious birds, different ranges of warblers, finches and southern variations of familiar European birds.

Mammals, as is normal, are rarely seen. Wild boar *(sus scrofa)* is common like the badger *(meles meles)*. The protected *cabra montes (capra pyrenaica)* is an ibex common in the Sierra Nevada and occasionally seen at village level. The male in particular is a majestic animal and well worth seeing.

Scorpions *(buthus occitanus)* are common, so we don't recommend walking in sandals.

Whatever your knowledge of botany there is no doubt that you will enjoy the abundance of wild flowers in spring from February to June depending on altitude. The zone of special scientific interest is that at an altitude of 3000m upwards where the combination of tundra conditions and warm Mediterranean air creates a zone unique in the world with a great many endemic species. Specialists in orchids and aromatic herbs will also find lots to interest them at lower levels.

The variety is what creates the interest, nature is constantly exploring the possible. The presence of a spring or a bit of shade can create a bit of Wales in the Mediterranean.

Historical Backgound

As with the geology so with the cultures; Africa and the Middle East fought Europe over Andalucia. They have all visited and left their mark in one way or another: the Phoenicians, Greeks ancient and modern, Celts, Romans, Visigoths and Arabs. The current incumbents are European Christians, the common perception being that of a re-conquest of Christianity over Islam after an absence of eight centuries. This simple view of a power struggle between religions is more realistically replaced by that of a rise and fall of the Islamic state of Al-Andalus which, for much of its history, was a loose collection of fiefdoms under an Islamic banner. Incursions from North Africa and other parts of the peninsular were frequent and even within the Muslim zone, local rulers were not averse to allying themselves with Christians for political and territorial gain. Granada and a few other neighbouring provinces hung on under Islam for so long, probably because they aided the Christians in the taking of Sevilla and Western Andalucia in the late 13th century.

Ultimately there was religious persecution and the 16th century saw a final drastic ethnic cleansing of Jews and Muslims from the state of Granada and from their last refuge, The Alpujarra.

After its forcible de-population, The Alpujarra was forcibly re-populated by peoples from all regions of Spain. What we see in The Alpujarra today is the product of what these immigrants from other regions and their descendants have made of it.

Virtually nothing remains in a physical sense of the Arab civilisation. Some fortress sites, some *acequias*, some architectural styles, and a fair amount of vocabulary and place names. "Constructed on the site of" are words one repeatedly reads in local history; in the context of ethnic cleansing it is easy to imagine the 'destruction' which preceded the 'construction'.

Culture, agriculture, economy and law were all replaced with new systems which, to judge by population growth, were successful up until the middle of the twentieth century. In this period of starvation, political persecution and industrial revolution, The Alpujarra, in common with much of rural Spain, experienced another de-population as its people fled to live or work in industrial Spain, France, Germany or Hispano America. The abandoned villages cre-

A corner of Bubión

ated are now visible and many more have decreased in size to the extent that they are not viable communities, while others are being re-populated by an influx of immigrants from Northern Europe, young Spaniards seeking the simple ecological way of life, or the elderly to spend their pensions. This is the reverse of what occurred 50 years ago. More signs of life are coming from the sons and grand-sons of those who fled. Now, some of those, too, want to re-build their ruined family homes and at least to use them as holiday retreats. All this suggests that the economy is increasingly tourism based, hence books such as this. Agriculture continues of course, but needs subsi-dising more, to prevent increasing amounts of land being abandoned. The charming view of unmechanised agriculture we have as tourists is a somewhat immoral and condescending view when we all expect cheap fruit and vegetables in a perfect state on the supermarket shelves, regardless of season. At the moment we are seeing the fading away of the last generation of noble peasant farmers in the region. An ironic situation when the modern view is that of a return to long term sustainable methods. So come and see the quaint before it ain't.

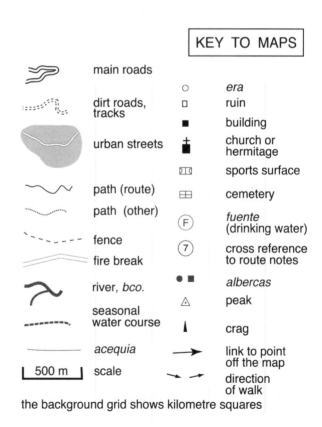

KEY TO MAPS

main roads	○ *era*
dirt roads, tracks	□ ruin
	■ building
urban streets	✝ church or hermitage
	ⵉⵉ sports surface
path (route)	⊞ cemetery
path (other)	Ⓕ *fuente* (drinking water)
fence	⑦ cross reference to route notes
fire break	● ■ *albercas*
river, *bco.*	△ peak
seasonal water course	▮ crag
acequia	→ link to point off the map
500 m scale	⤵ direction of walk

the background grid shows kilometre squares

The Poqueira Valley: Pampaneira, Bubión, and Capileira

Fact File

Medical Emergency: Doctor's consulting rooms in Pampaneira. Nearest 24hr emergency centre is in Pitres (10 minutes by car).

Buses: the villages are on the Granada – Alcutar route. Three buses in and out each day. Bubión and Capileira being on a dead end road the buses in each direction take the same route. See Appendix A for times.

Accommodation: Lots. A selection is given in Appendix B.

Shops: Everything you could expect in small villages and more nick-nack shops than the wallet can bear.

Banks: Automatic cash machines in each village and a bank in Capileira.

Restaurants: Yes, many. Mentioning a couple: La Artesa (Bubión) – quality Spanish food at a reasonable price. Ibero fusion (Capileira) – eclectic menu, including vegetarian.

Bars: Bodega (Pampaneira – downhill from the church square), a great place to test the wine and do all your present buying simultaneously. Ciber Monfi (Bubión – see sketch map), nice for variety, Moroccan tea, sweets and snacks, also functions as cyber-café.
Bar Tilo (Capileira), hospitable bar, good *tapas* and *raciónes*.

The three villages of the Poqueira Valley differ very much in character; Pampaneira is unashamedly commercial and concentrates on catching the passing trade. It is not the best place to stay from a point of view of walking but it does have a perfect *plaza* for dining out in, and offers more 'life' than any other village in The Alpujarra.

The information centre in Pampaneira's *plaza* is run as a private enterprise by Nevandensis (Appendix E). A visit to their exhibition is a must at some time during your visit.

The best selection of the quality foods of The Alpujarra can be seen in the bodega in c. Veronica and this is a useful place to buy a present for who ever is looking after the budgie, or indeed for Joey himself. If you have not yet acclimatised your palate to *vino costa* this is also a good place to start, or try again while you ponder over suitable gifts.

None of the walks specifically include Pampaneira but an old mule path is easily followed between Bubión and Pampaneira – see village plans.

Bubión is the most reserved of the Poqueira villages, perhaps the quietest and least entertaining of them. It houses the office of 'Rustic Blue' (Appendix E) who are English speaking and may be of use in the planning of your holiday in advance. Bubión also has the best museum of local life and culture to be found in The Alpujarra. *Casa Alpujarreña*, Museo Municipal is in Plaza Iglesia at the lower end of the village. It provides a really interesting visit, mornings only, closed Tuesday.

Capileira is the best place to stay from a point of view of access to the walks, particularly Walk 2. Walk 1 gives a guided tour of the village itself.

The Poqueira Gorge has spoken for itself and become *the* centre for tourism to The Alpujarra. It has attracted Spanish trippers for many years but more recently the area has been promoted worldwide.

The villages themselves get very busy, particularly at weekends; if your accommodation is in the village centre you might have to lose some sleep and adapt to the nocturnal lifestyle of the Spanish on holiday.

It is not for nothing that the visitors come – the valley is spectacular and the villages take pride in showing themselves off. As far as walkers are concerned, the weekend crowds need not be a problem. They are easily avoided by going midweek or by walking a few hundred metres out of the village. All the activity makes a welcome change after the concentrated peace of The Alpujarra as a whole.

Many businesses, information offices etc. are exhausted by Sunday night, breathe a sigh of relief and don't open on Monday.

Local guides and the authorities have collaborated to set up eight waymarked routes and large wooden information boards to publicise them. A map and book (see kit list) describe the routes and provides and good map of the area.

The routes described below do not rely on any waymarks but many will be seen. They are not generally mentioned in the **Notes**. The routes described vary in length from 1 hour strolls to a picnic spot, to two-day treks to the highest mountain in mainland Spain. They show the best of the valley with the minimum of problems.

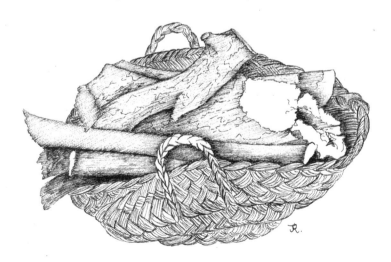

1. Capileira Village Stroll

Time: 2½ hours including visits.

Notes: Never leaves the village. Best done between mid-morning and lunchtime (2pm) to make sure everything is open and functioning. On Mondays and Tuesdays some establishments close and so it may be best to plan around that.

1. Start at the kiosk, newsagent/information centre on the main road. Walk uphill a few metres and fork left past Hostal Meson Poqueira. At the junction ahead go left, downhill into Plaza Calvario where sits the bar El Tilo in the shade of its lime tree.

2. There is good drinking water at the fuente in Plaza Calverio. Make your way downhill into the adjoining plaza where the church is and take c. Real from its upper left corner.

    Before following c. Real downhill have a look at the peaceful c. Duende and wonder who or what lived here.

    On the downhill section of c. Real is a little courtyard filled with flowers and greenery. You would think it to be a little over the top. Apart from the pleasure of having the plants, there is a practical reason for so much greenery. You can feel the cooling effect that so many leaves have, by virtue of their transpiration. You notice the same effect when walking into a tree-filled gully, the temperature drops noticeably over and above the effect of shade.

    Join c. Escuelas and turn left, then right into c. Mentidero on the edge of the village with the valley at its feet.

    The museum 'Museo Alpujarreño de Pedro Antonio de Alarcón' is in c. Mentidero and is worth a quick visit. A small charge is made and the door is usually shut even during its open hours. Knock and you will be let in. Pedro Antonio de Alarcón was a 19th-century poet and writer who visited The Alpujarra and wrote what has become one of the classic travel books on the area. The book is for sale in all the gift/book shops and it is interesting to get a 100-year-old romantic's view.

    As far as exhibits go perhaps the ones most worth seeing are the tools and implements housed in what were stables on the ground floor. There are interesting items relating to agriculture, woodwork, fabrics and weaving.

    The wooden sledge-type things under the wooden pitch forks are what were and are used to thresh on the eras and the wooden boxes are standard measures of grain by volume.

    The wooden forks are particularly appealing; grown in one piece, from the almez tree (celtis australis) which tends to branch with various shoots from the same point and then helped with a bit of training

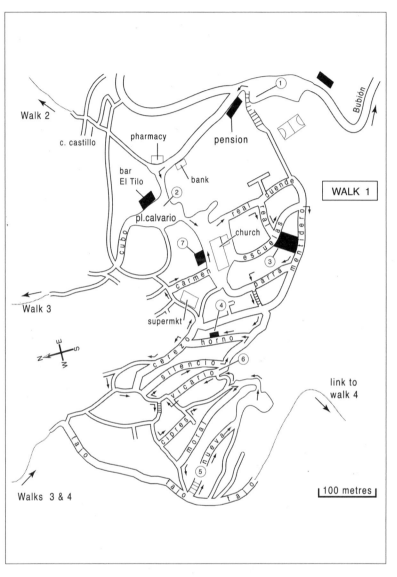

and pruning. You might grow a new fork in three or four years so think ahead and look for a suitable tree if you think you might need one.

The joiner's bench too, is special but not unique. They occasionally turn up in *cortijos* still occupied by older people. The hand carving of threads like these must have been a skill much in demand. The grape and olive presses, of which there would have been hundreds, used to have a wooden screw thread of much greater diameter than these, of olive or chestnut timber. (See also the museum house in Bubión church square).

3. From the front door of the museum turn right into c. Parra and left past restaurant Ibero Fusion, one of the very few places where vegetarians are catered for.

At the crossroads go straight over, down the steps into c. Horno. Keep on the level c. Horno until passing the bakers sign, Horno de Luisa.

You must go into the baker's on the pretext of buying something. You will see the huge dome of the brick oven, this is pre-heated with firewood and the dough put in when the fire has done its job and died down. The ash is scraped to the back and the dough put in to cook.

The large wooden trough to the left of the counter is an artesa, you will have seen one in the museum. This is standard equipment for hand mixing large quantities of food, in this case bread dough.

If you just want a normal long thin loaf ask for, una barra, [oo-na ba-rra]. Another good choice if you want a bread that keeps longer is pan de aceite, [pan day a-thay-i-tay], bread with olive oil in which sometimes comes with a sugar coating.

With luck, Luisa may be shovelling the bread out of the oven with that great long-handled spatula as you arrive.

4. Turn right as you leave the bread shop. Follow the road leftish and down, c. Cerezo.

Part way down c. Cerezo when in sight of a flower bedecked balcony on a bend lower down, take the alley to the right. It is a nice cool alley with a shady *tinao* for each house. It curls round to the left. Keep turning left and rejoin c. Cerezo on the bend just below the flower strewn, triangular, balcony.

Turn right and downhill, take the steps down to the right. Pass more flowery corners and follow the road around to the left to enter c. Fuente Cipres.

You may have noticed mysterious hanging polythene bags of water and polythene bottles of water around doorsteps and flowerpots. These, I am assured, are to ward off two different sorts of pests: flies and urinating dogs. We are left to wonder how they work but the experience is that they do; perhaps in both cases, on taking an initial sniff they are frightened away by a huge reflection!

Continue along c. Cipres and take a right turn into c. Moral and follow it to its end at the very bottom of the village. c. Tajo or cliff street for obvious reasons.

c. Tajo followed to its extreme, passes out of the bottom of the village towards the south. It becomes a path leading down to the river at puente molino and provides a link with Walk 4.

5. From c. Tajo take the steps up into c. Neuva and follow it along to the little *plaza*, *fuente*, and below the square to the right the

wash-house where you can imagine the echoing of many tongues out across the valley. It is certainly a wash-house with a view.

Leaving the *fuente* on the left pass out of the *plaza* up and left. Keep to the right and turn right, up the steps under the low, covered, alley (*tinao*) that zigzags up to join c. Vicario to the left.

6. c. Vicario is worth finding and enjoying. At the end of c. Vicario is a hairpin right into c. Silencio. It always has been when I have visited, so perhaps it is the custom to keep it that way.

Turn left at the end of c. Silencio, to c. Horno. Another chance to visit the bread shop if you missed it on the way down.

Turn left to pass the baker's and right at the end of the street, uphill. There is quite a nice dead-end alley, c. Quinque, on the left just before the *fuente*. Pass the *fuente* and go left uphill, passing the supermarket. After the supermarket branch right into c. *Carmen* which leads to the church.

7. Turn left, uphill at the end of c. Carmen and look for Bodega La Alacena within a few metres.

After climbing up from the bottom of the village you deserve a sit down in pleasant surroundings. Pass through the tiny shop of the bodega, full of interesting local food produce, and take a seat in the back room. In summer it's cool and in winter a fire burns. The room speaks for itself and so will the wine; you may not like what it says but it's worth a try. Vino costa joven, [beano costa hob-en] is my favourite but in the interests of a full investigation you should try the aged version, vino viejo, [beano vee-eh-hoe], or the sweet version which goes down easily on a cold day, vino dulce, [beano dull-thay].

I like the aged, stained furniture as much as anything else here. The construction of the tables is typical of those seen in every old house that hasn't been improved with chipboard and Formica.

The chairs too; often they are apparently ridiculously low or made for children. The reality is that they are not made for sitting at tables but for performing tasks on the floor with a bucket between your feet, or for cooking over the fire in the hearth, for which they are eminently suitable.

Enjoy your wine and find your own way back to the start point of the walk, it is uphill.

2. Capileira – Mulhacén – Capileira

The walk is intended as an access route to Refugio Poqueira (Appendix B), a hostel at 2500m providing an excellent base for peak-baggers or walkers who want to experience the Sierra Nevada in relative comfort and safety. The route enables an ascent to the hostel on day one, exploration on subsequent days and descent by a different route described in the **Notes**.

A circular day walk is possible by omitting the last leg of the walk to the hostel. The walk is best undertaken in late spring, as soon as the snow has retreated to above 2500m, or at anytime throughout the summer, when temperatures are mitigated by the altitude and mountain winds. *Bco. Mulhacén* above the hostel is a magic place which I would love you to see, dotted with *lagunas* and pouring water from dozens of springs, it makes a fantastic place to spend a summer's day. In this summery daydream we must include the fact of being on a serious mountain where a summer's day could also include cloud, gales, rain and hail so please go prepared.

Times: Circular route omitting the hostel, 7½ to 10 hours including rests; Capileira to hostel 6 to 8 hours including rests; Hostel to Capileira 4½ to 6 hours including rests.

Waymarks: Many waymarks will be passed but none are specifically followed.

Find out from the information centre in Pampaneira, at what height snow is lying. The paths are well used and clear throughout but not with snow on them. This is a hard walk by any standards, see profile diagram, it climbs at least 1000m (circular option) in 9km and should not be undertaken by anyone uncertain of their fitness for this amount of climbing.

Users of this route should be aware of the normal safety and survival procedures that apply when walking in remote areas at high altitude.

---

1. Leave Capileira by c. Castillo, see map 1, a cobbled road leaving the village to the north. Within 50m of the last houses, c. Castillo crosses another village track and continues as a cobbled path.

    Very soon after leaving the village the river bed falls away as the path climbs and the amazing extent of the ancient terracing can be seen. Particularly impressive is that on the east of the river where the slopes are steeper. Mostly unused and abandoned now except for roaming flocks of sheep and goats, it can only be imagined as it was in earlier times of higher population and greater utilisation.

2. The path passes by two tiny concrete sheds before meeting a track

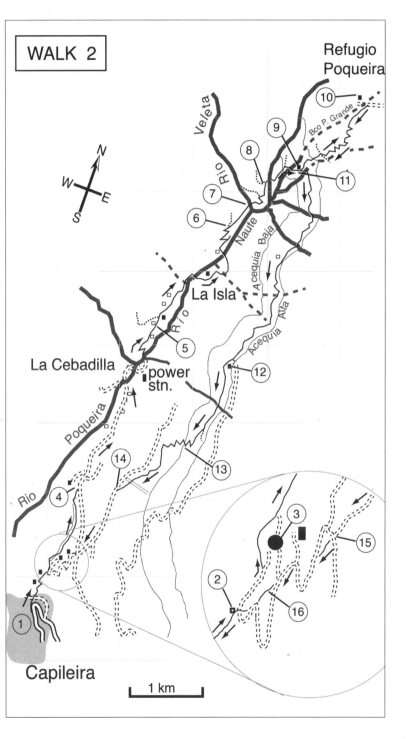

coming down from above. It is worth noting the second of these to help find the path on the descent. Turn left along the track and 200m later, fork down, left to pass just below a circular water installation (3).

The path crosses an *acequia* and continues obviously on to join the vehicle access road to the hydro-electric power plant at La Cebadilla.

4. Turn left and follow the track towards the power station.

Taking advantage of this easy section to look around gives the rather daunting sight of Mulhacén (NNE) and on a plateau half way up, the Refugio Poqueira with its red roofs where, no doubt, they have got the kettle on ready.

50m after joining the track ignore a right branch, continue downhill. 50m later ignore a minor track going hairpin left. Pass through the abandoned workers village of La Cebadilla, cross the river bridge and turn right.

Follow the concrete road past the power station, to its end at another bridge. Follow the path which heads off, right on the far side of the bridge.

At the top of this steep zigzag section, on the level section that follows, are some left uphill options to ignore. The route continues to follow the line of the valley Río Naute (NNE).

Pass a small ruin on the right and arrive at another on the left.

5. In sight is a white-painted *cortijo* a few hundred metres ahead on the right. At this junction of paths keep right towards the *cortijo*, following the valley. Pass above the *cortijo* and then below two others before descending, crossing a minor tributary, to the river bed.

The path uses various small stone bridges to find its way through the river and past the aptly named *Cortijo La Isla*.

Follow the path on its slight diversion on the east bank to cross a tributary coming down from the right and then cross to the west bank by another bridge.

The path zigzags up. Ignore a minor right part way up the zigzags. At the top of the zigzags follow the line of the river, ignoring a left branch (6). Between here and the bridge at the river junction (7), the path passes many springs and tends to disappear beneath verdant growth. It is never very difficult to follow and stays as close as it can to the river.

At this bridge (7) is the junction of two rivers with very significant names in the Sierra Nevada. They are named after the two highest peaks of the range and they draw their waters from the snows melting on the southern slopes of Veleta and Mulhacén. Veleta is a sharp shark's-tooth shape as seen from the south and its name means 'weather vane'. Mulhacén is named after an Emir of Granada, Muley Hacén. He wished on his death for his heart to be buried in a place he loved and in which it would never be disturbed. In choosing Mulhacén as such a place he couldn't have been expected to predict the extent of modern tourism and the hundreds of feet that tramp over his heart on this now very accessible mountain.

The Río Mulhacén is joined near the bridge (7), by a confusing multitude of tributary *barrancos* some carrying water, others not, depending on season and conditions. The route described crosses to the east side of Río Mulhacén and stays between it and Bco. Peñón Negro for the remainder of its way to the refuge.

7. Once across the bridge the path is between the rivers Veleta and Mulhacén. 20m after the bridge ignore any left turn that goes to recross the Río Veleta. The path, via a zigzag devious course tends to follow the more easterly Mulhacén water course.

    On a bearing of about 40 degrees from here can be seen what appears to be a ruin but is the, as yet used, *cortijo* of Las Tomas which is the next target to aim for.

8. At the dividing of ways take the right option which goes on to cross the Río Mulhacén in the gully immediately to the east.

    The path zigzags around on the shoulder of the hill at first near the *barranco* coming down from Las Tomas and then on the east bank of Río Mulhacén. Eventually settling for the more easterly small *barranco* it passes a ruined corral and then meets *Acequia Baja*.

    Just on the upper side of the *acequia* is a division of paths. This route heads right, NE to cross the small *barranco* and zigzags the last few hundred metres to Cortijo Las Tomas above (9).

    Most of us on arriving at Las Tomas will be tired to put it mildly. A lot depends on the weather, in hot weather climbing up the river valleys where there is no freshening wind can be quite exhausting. At least now we can see why we are tired; the villages have been left way below and hidden by bends in the valley. It is a satisfying sight and a beautiful area to dawdle through. The zone from below the Acequia Baja through Las Tomas to the Acequia Alta above is much damper than neighbouring zones, outside of the influence of the *acequias*. The verdant growth of herbs, grasses and flowering plants attracts all we animal forms of life to take advantage of it to eat, rest, mate, bathe and move on refreshed.

Las Tomas is the point of decision for those who are prepared for both options of this walk. A tired person could take 2 hours (uphill) to reach the hostel. To complete the circular walk back to the village will take about 1 hour less than taken to come up to Las Tomas. If following the circular walk continue from point (11) in the Notes.

9. At Las Tomas *Cortijo* there is a junction of paths. If it has survived there is a wooden sign pointing the way (NE) up the hill towards the Refugio Poqueira. It is a well-trodden path, which heads up the shoulder of the hill between the *barrancos Peñon Grande* and *Peñon Negro* on about 60°.

   Cross *Acequia Alta* at 2200m leaving 300m to climb over the last 1.5km of the route.

   Cross a path running around the contour, continue up on about 60°. The path curves around to the north to zigzag up the last steep section before emerging onto the plateau where sits the hostel, a few hundred metres away. In bad visibility follow the gully just to the left of the path, or the path itself until it meets the track leading to the refuge.

   I abandon you to your own devices at the hostel. What you do depends as much on season and weather as your own inclinations. The obvious choice for most people is an ascent of Mulhacén but it involves a lot of tramping over hot bare rock, or snow. An equally satisfying view can be obtained from the lesser target of the ridge above the lagunas, at the top of Río Mulhacén. Even if you do ascend Mulhacén I insist that you include the Río Mulhacén somewhere in your route. In this way the 'hard' will be mitigated by the 'green and pleasant'. Another option would be to contour round to the east of Mulhacén to arrive at Las Siete Lagunas, another special place described under chapter Trevelez, Walk 10.

Descent: Refugio Poqueira to Capileira

10. From the track 100m east of the refuge, a gully heads down across the plateau at about 255°. The path follows it on the same route used by the ascent.

   As the terrain gets steeper the path diverges left from the gully and zigzags down. Visibility permitting Cortijo Las Tomas comes into sight 1km away on 240°. On this stretch the path crosses a contouring path and then *Acequia Alta* to arrive at the *cortijo (9)*.

11. At the junction of paths on the east of the buildings follow the branch east into the *bco*.

   There follow four or five relatively easy kilometres as the well used path winds around the contours between the Acequias Alta and Baja. At one point the path rises to meet Acequia Alta and from here you can best appreciate an impressive jumble of peaks in the middle distance and on the skyline, as the saw toothed ridges of the Sierra cut the sky from Veleta to Mulhacén. The two huge bowls below the two main peaks, originally cut by glaciers of an early ice age have subsequently been sub-divided by lesser glaciations and weathering, into a confusion of peaks and *barrancos* big and small. The refuge can be seen sitting on its plateau created by the dumping of debris at the snout of an early large glacier in its retreat. The *lagunas* sit invisible, higher up in their hanging valleys, created in a similar way by the dumping of debris from smaller more recent glaciers. The remnants of a glacier existed until the early 20th century.

12. From *Cortijo* Corrales de Pitres, identified by the track that runs down to it, the path continues more or less level for a while then dips into a *barranco*. It climbs quite steeply out of the *barranco* across a grey/black earthy scree.

A few hundred metres after the climb there is a fork in the path. Take the right, slightly downhill option.

13. Cross *Acequia Baja* and continue to zigzag down on the lower side. A line of conifers is now visible ahead. The path levels then zigzags down under green lichen-covered cliffs.

On meeting the fire break, running up and down the hill along the edge of the pines, cross it to follow the continuing path through the trees on the other side.

14. At the track turn left to follow it. At the next track junction take the right fork downhill.

15. At the junction of tracks go straight over and follow the track south downhill.

After passing the turn to a new stone-built goat coral, look for a path leaving the track on the right.

16. This leads down towards the tiny concrete shed (2), which marks the start of the path leading down to Capileira.

3. Capileira and the River

An evening or before breakfast walk maybe; equally a short walk to a long picnic by the river.

Time: 2 hours plus picnic time

Worth doing to get a sight of a somewhat inaccessible and luxuriant part of the valley on the opposite bank.

1. Start at Plaza Calvario in Capileira , see map 1.

    Fill up with drinking water at the *fuente* in the *plaza* then leaving the *fuente* on the right, follow c. Cubo out of the *plaza*. Turn right at the T-junction.

    A left and a right in quick succession lead to a paved road leaving the village on the contour more or less.

2. The paved road leads out of the village to the north, passes two *eras* side by side that are now normally used as car parks.

    A broad well-used path continues on the contour or gently down. Ignore any minor paths to left or right. The path crosses a *barranco*, 50m later, ignore a minor path to the right.

3. Take a hairpin left just before arriving at a large ruin, a few metres off the path to the right. Four or five sets of zigzags lead steeply down the cobbled path.

    A good path joins from the left and the route continues north and north west curving around the head of a *barranco* below, and under a cliff above.

    Pass a ruin on the immediate right of the path. A few more zigzags down a beautiful path, part bedrock, part cobbled lead to the bridge (4).

    There is plenty of shade here and water from the river to enable you to picnic or just sit comfortably. If it's a cold day and more exercise is appropriate, then following the path north west from the far side of the bridge puts you on a waymarked route to La Cebadilla and back to Capileira in about 2½ hours.

4. When ready to return to Capileira, retrace steps up from the river bridge, and look out for the ruin passed on the left of the path.

5. A few hundred metres after passing the ruin look for a good path forking right. Following this path to the right leads around to Cortijo de la Sacristia.

    Pass around above the *cortijo* and join another good path climbing up from the river to Capileira.

6. Turn left and follow the clear path back into the village.

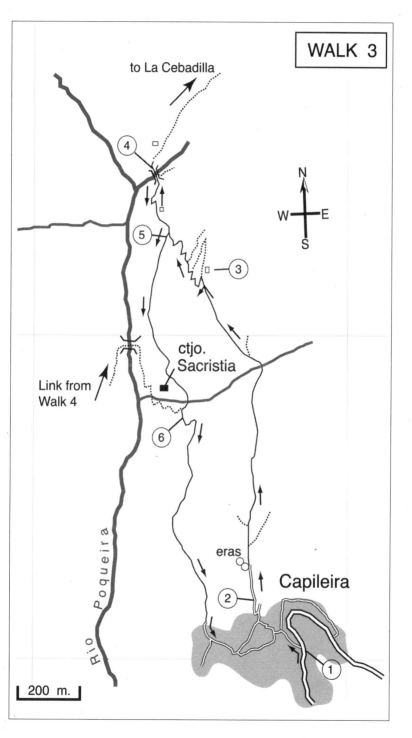

WALK 3

to La Cebadilla

④

N
W — E
S

⑤

③

ctjo.
Sacristia

Link from
Walk 4

⑥

Río Poqueira

eras

Capileira

②

①

200 m.

The route enters Capileira very near the lowest point of the village c. Tajo (see map 1). If you have not already done Walk 1 this may be a good opportunity to explore the village. Start at point (5) on map 1 and follow the Notes for Walk 1.

A little door in Capileira

4. Bubión – River Valley – Capileira – Bubión

Time: 3½ hours plus any time spent in Capileira

Notes: A relatively easy walk, albeit with two climbs out of the valley bottom. Taken slowly it will be completed in the time stated. The *Puente Molino*, 45 minutes out of Bubión village, makes a good place for those who only want a short walk, picnic and snooze. The path is clearly visible throughout the route.

1. Start in Bubión at the main road where Bar Teide and Bar Artesa face each other across the road. Go down about 20m and turn right on the road passing just below the car park.

   Aiming for the church, turn left at the wash-house down c. Lavadero. Take a right turn into c. Parras and then a left down-hill.

   Turn right at the T-junction to arrive at the church. Leave the church square by c. Real past the museum house. Follow this road as it leaves the village. It leads on down to the sports ground.

2. Turn right at the shrine and pass below the sports ground. Follow the obvious path into barranco Tejar, where it passes under some grand walnut trees and crosses the stream by bridge.

   Just as you leave the *barranco* a path branches right but follow the main path left as it zigzags steeply down. Pass a large ruin just to the left of the path.

   The path enters another shady *barranco* and crosses the water by bridge. Just after this bridge is a path branching hairpin right. Ignore this unless wanting to go directly to Capileira. Follow the main path downhill through some steep zigzags to the *Puente Molino* (3).

3. Cross the river by the bridge and follow the path as it zigzags up to a T-junction of paths alongside a bridge over the stream.

4. Turn right without crossing the bridge. The path heads north, gradually climbing, until it reaches a working *cortijo* (5).

   The elderly man who works away here is friendly and talkative. He is one of a dying breed who persist, against all the trends, in living on and from the land. He probably has a modern home in the village, but like others of his type seems to prefer to live in the same place and in the same way, with the same lack of facilities as he has done throughout his 3 score and 10.

   If you are enticed in to visit his kingdom, don't leave your rucksack unattended; his dogs seem to have learnt that walkers have picnics and are expert at extracting anything edible from them. Apart from

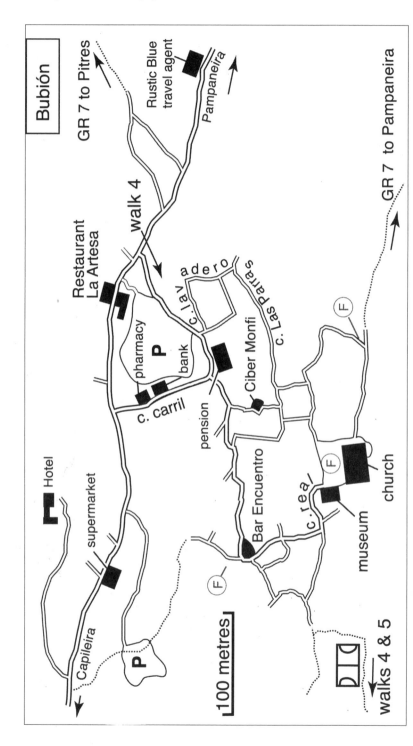

Bubión

GR 7 to Pitres

Rustic Blue
travel agent

Pampaneira

GR 7 to Pampaneira

walk 4

Restaurant
La Artesa

c. lavadero

c. Las Parras

pharmacy

P

bank

Ciber Monfi

c. carril

pension

Hotel

supermarket

Bar Encuentro

c. rea

museum

church

Capileira

P

100 metres

F

walks 4 & 5

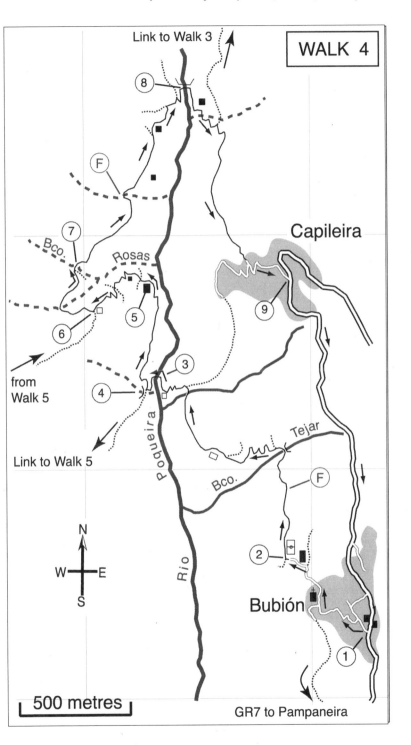

being a breeder of robber dogs this gentleman has other surprising talents that go to show how deceptive appearances can be. He is a musician, playing, and teaching in the past, the local traditional *bandurria*, a 12-stringed lute-like instrument. He is also the provider of one of my favourite good answers to silly questions from walkers: on seeing about 20 identical sickles hanging on his kitchen wall I asked,

"Why do you have so many?"

"I've got a lot of land."

Bandurria

5. The path passes to the right of the *cortijo*. 100m after the *cortijo*, cross a vague path/acequia, and continue climbing. The path zig-zags up and passes a disused *cortijo* on the left.

Capileira comes into sight, sitting on its cliff on the opposite side of the valley, and the path arrives at an *era*. The path zigzags right, away from the *era,* and immediately crosses another vague path/*acequia* and continues up the shoulder of the hill. Continue climbing and within 500m the path passes a stone built, disused *alberca* with an overgrown ruin and *era* above it.

6. There is a division of paths a few metres past the *alberca*. Take the right fork down into the *barranco*, and cross on the bridge.

7. At the next *barranco* a path joins from the right and both cross together over the bridge. The path divides and rejoins itself a few metres later.

    Another *barranco* is crossed and the path continues obviously onward. It passes around the back of a white-painted *cortijo*. Ignore any minor paths to the left. Continue on the most obvious path, tending downhill to arrive at the river again.

8. From the bridge the path takes a south east course and is easily followed to Capileira about 1km away. Take any route uphill through Capileira to arrive at the main road.

    If you want to extend your time in Capileira use the information contained in Walk 1.

    There is no convenient off-road route from Capileira to Bubión and so this route uses the main road.

9. Turn right down the main road and arrive in Bubión after about 1.5km.

5. Bubión – O Sel ing – Bubión

The nominal target of the walk is the Buddhist retreat and study centre set up as a result of the reincarnation of a llama as a young boy, resident in Bubión. The walk is very worthwhile for any reason. Between points (9) and (11), the track provides very easy walking and a chance to stretch the legs and enjoy great views in both directions. If time and tides have taken their toll and you don't feel up to the whole walk it is possible to drive to point (9), by following the sketch map. You could then enjoy the easy section between (9) and (11).

Time: 5 hours plus rests and visiting time. Easily shortened by 2 hours if the section between (7) and (10) is omitted. If the walk is being done with a view to visiting O Sel ing, bear in mind that visitors are received between 3pm and 6pm and the walk back to Bubión takes 3 hours.

Notes: The first and last sections of this walk are shown in more detail on map 4.

Difficulties: No water and very little shade between points (4) and (10). Carry water for the return trip.

1. From Bubión church square follow c. Real past the museum house 'Casa Alpujarreña', and out of the village to the north. The paved road fades to a path as it leads to the sports pitches.

2. Turn right at the shrine to pass the pitches and follow the clear path into *Barranco* Tejar, crossing the stream by the bridge. Continue down the zigzag path ignoring any minor right turns.

   Cross the waters of another *barranco*. Ignore a branch path, hairpin right and continue down the zigzags to the river bridge, *Puente Molino*.

3. Cross the river and after about 100m arrive at the T-junction of paths.

4. Turn left crossing the waters of the *barranco*. The path continues steeply now, still easily followed. There are some minor right turns to ignore before passing into a tree-filled *barranco* and crossing its stream.

   The path emerges from an area of oaks into a clearing and now only gently climbing, crosses a meadow in front of a ruined, two-storey *cortijo* (5).

5. Ignore any waymarks that may exist here. The route continues from the northern corner of the ruin and angles uphill to the north west. Continue following the most obvious path as it curls around the side of another ruin (6).

6. Ignore a right branch, the route curls around the ruin to continue its uphill course now to the south.

Among the consequences of there being so many abandoned farmsteads is one good one for us as walkers: the scrumping is good. On this route in the right season it is possible to take advantage of the fruit trees planted by previous generations but now mostly abandoned by this. Cherries, figs, mulberries, plums, blackberries, chestnuts and walnuts all offer their produce. The ruin (6) has some particularly good figs if you pass in August.

The path continues to join a track (7).

7. Turn left along the track. There are minor turns, one to the right and another to the left before arriving at a T-junction.

8. Turn left at the T-junction and about 1km later arrive at a junction where a sign points the way, right to O Sel ing, the Buddhist centre.

9. If visiting O Sel ing turn right.

10. Descending from O Sel ing arrive at the junction of tracks (9), where there are signs and information boards.

9. Turn hairpin left to follow the same track as on the outwards walk but now in a northerly direction.

Around about here there is quite a different view from any seen in the other walks. The valley below to the south east is that of Río Guadalfeo and from here we look down into a broad gravely bed at the point where all the rivers of the western Alpujarra join. The Río Poqueira joins the Río Trevelez, out of sight at our feet and together they join the Río Guadalfeo. The broad gravel bed of the Guadalfeo narrows as it rises eastwards through the narrow gorge of Puerto de Juviléy. The Sierra de Juviléy is that island of crags which lately has been shaved along its crown to make a fire break. This line of the fire break is also the line of civil war trenches, many of which can still be found silently guarding the main passes. This area of Puerto de Juviléy is dealt with by a walk in the chapter of miscellaneous walks.

Ignore a branch track descending to the right and continue on the main track following the contour. It passes a vineyard on the left then a goat corral and another *cortijo* on the right.

8. At this track junction take the downhill option to the right and after about 50m ignore a right branch.

Pass a group of two or three buildings just below the track and very soon after, a *cortijo* above the track on the left. 0.5km later arrive at (7), where the track bends left and a clear path, used on the outward part of the walk, joins the track from the right.

The abundance of cortijos in this area, both abandoned and in use, together with the rare sight of so much flat land, so many *eras*, and so many *albercas* makes it easy to imagine what a hive of activity there must have been in this area. The *albercas* are not visible concrete structures, but are usually natural depressions of terrain with a stone-built retaining wall around the lower edge to level off a water catchment area whose size and shape is dependent on the lie of the land. At the lowest point a stone tunnel is built into this wall and under the structure to taper to a plug-hole. Because this plug-hole is out of arm's reach a variety of devices are found for plugging and unplugging. Usually a long pole, tapered to fit the tunnel is found nearby. The waterproofing of the *alberca* is simply a lining of soil. Some good examples of these organic, low-tech reservoirs can be found slightly above and below the track south of (7). In passing through this terrain it is worth remembering that in the 19th century the population of The Alpujarra was triple what it is today and that communications being what they were, the area had to be self-sufficient.

7. Head north west on the track. After about 30m ignore a minor track left. A few hundred metres later a branch left leads only to a renovated *cortijo*. This *cortijo* enjoys a splendid walnut tree growing fat on a spring that spills out nearby. Continue on the main track, passing behind another *cortijo* 100m later.

11. The track, having deteriorated to a path, arrives at the head of a dry gully. The path crosses the gully and begins its descent, at first gentle, then very steep, towards the river.

    The path is clear but much divided as users make their own varied zigzags down. It keeps to the shoulder of the hill with a *barranco* to the left and right.

12. On a hairpin bend there is a junction of paths. Turn right down the shoulder of the hill, eastwards, aiming for the cliff on which Capileira can be seen sitting.

    Turning left at (12), would be to join Walk 4 and arrive at Capileira after about 1 hour's walking.

    Immediately after (12), there is a stone and earth *alberca* on the right. Four or five zigzags of the path lead down to a ruin on the immediate right. Cross a minor path and continue down the zigzags, passing an *era*. More zigzags lead down to pass to the left of a *cortijo*.

    The architectural style of this *cortijo* has not yet reached the text books. I would say that it is very typical of the area's style, not in terms of its end result but in terms of the principle behind it. This being that of; use what is available. There is no clay in the area, therefore no roof-tiles, therefore flat roofs. But there is stone, earth, wooden poles, bamboo and in this case – mattresses.

    Follow the obvious path as it leads down from the *cortijo*.

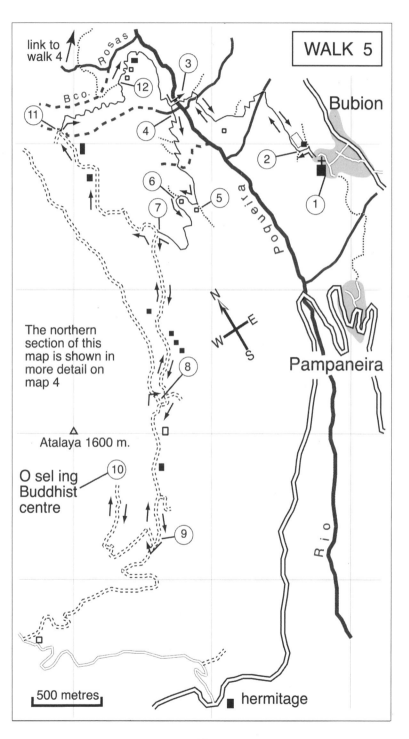

WALK 5

link to walk 4

Bubion

The northern section of this map is shown in more detail on map 4

△ Atalaya 1600 m.

O sel ing Buddhist centre

Pampaneira

Rio

500 metres

hermitage

4. At the junction of paths at the mini-bridge in the *barranco*, turn left without crossing the bridge. 100m later cross the river on the bridge and follow the stone path rising in a downstream direction.

The path passes a branch to the left which leads to Capileira; keep to the right and cross a stream in the *barranco* by the bridge. From here it is 30 minutes slow walk uphill to Bubión. Follow the well-used path ignoring minor branches.

In Bubión take the first left, c. Hondillo and then the first right which leads to the doorstep of Bar Encuentro.

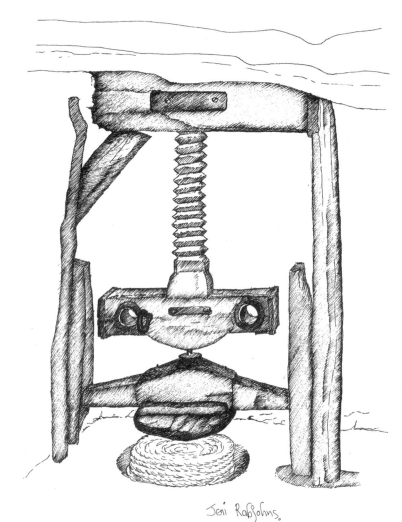

Wine press, Bubion

La Taha de Pitres

Fact File: La Taha de Pitres

Buses: They call at Pitres, Pórtugos and Busquístar. See Appendix A

Accommodation: Hotels in Pitres, Pórtugos and Mecina. A B&B in Ferreirola has the best location for the walker, is in the most beautiful setting, is run by walkers but you really need a car to use it. See Appendix B.

Shops: Pitres has the best selection but Busquístar and Pórtugos also have the essentials.

Bank: Pitres has a bank and cashpoint.

Restaurants: in Pitres, Pórtugos and Mecina. Notable is the novelty of a vegetarian restaurant in Spain; El Jardin in Pitres. Also Bar Sierra Nevada next to the supermarket in Pitres for interesting traditional food and ambience.

Medical Emergency: 24hr centre in Pitres town square. Pharmacies in Pitres and Pórtugos.

Taxi: Run by the "Coviran" supermarket in Pitres square. Ask in the shop or telephone 958 766055.

The word Taha comes from the Arabic for municipality but, in this case, the word has stuck and is used here for the area now controlled by Pitres. There are nine villages and hamlets, all of which are visited on the walks. The close proximity of the villages and the network of old paths that link them make this a great area to walk and the most "green and pleasant" of all The Alpujarra. It is famous for its springs, which in turn encourage plenty of trees for shade along the way.

Esparto cheese mould

6. Linking the main villages of La Taha (de Pitres)

The walk takes its starting point as Pórtugos. It has an '8'-shaped route which passes through all the villages which have lodgings. so it can be joined wherever is convenient. The knowledge gained on this walk will enable joining into Walks 7, 8 and 9 depending on which village is being used for accommodation. The main objective is a promontory known as La Mezquita, a historic site occupying a magical position from which the whole of this section of the Río Trevelez gorge can be surveyed. La Mezquita is also visited by Walk 7.

Time: The route is '8'-shaped. Starting at Pórtugos there are three possibilities: complete route: 5 to 7 hours including stops and lunch; points (1)-(13) – 2 to 3 hours; points (13) onwards – 2 to 3 hours.

Waymarks: The route coincides with parts of various waymarked routes but does not follow any particular one.

Difficulties: The path on La Mezquita has some big steps along it making it troublesome for the less agile. Some scratchy vegetation on the same stretch makes shorts a liability.

1. Start from the hotel on the main road through Pórtugos. Leave the village on the main road, going east in the direction of Busquístar. After a few hundred metres the road passes Fuente Agria.

   Fuente Agria attracts many visitors; some coming as pilgrims to visit the shrine to Our Lady, Virgin of Sorrows, some to take the waters, regarded as medicinal for the high contents of iron, calcium, magnesium and silica in the form of sulphates, carbonates and hydroxides. Others come to take the ice cream and walk down to the grotto just below the road, a good refreshing place on a hot day.

   Continue along the road for about 1km, looking out for a stone kilometre marker with 'L14' and 'km33' carved on it.

2. 50m after the 'km33' stone, take the track heading down, right from the bend in the road. 40m down the track fork right along the track or path which follow each other. Pass the metal pylon and go alongside the raspberry plantation.

3. Immediately before the track begins to descend turn left to follow the small *acequia* that passes between the two meadows on the ridge.

4. At the end of the meadows the path drops a little onto more rocky terrain and tending to the right continues following the ridge to the south.

   The rather scratchy scrub that does not much more than hinder most of the year, earns its keep during the spring. The holly oak decorates itself with long fat yellow catkins with dark red stamens, the gorse becomes bright yellow (and scratchy) and amongst it all the white and pink cistuses and rock roses make a spectacularly natural garden.

The path ends on the promontory near the ruin and era..

The obvious ruin is relatively modern but closer examination of the site can reveal various signs of earlier occupations. There are many flat areas of rock that have been carved out and above some of them, holes in the cliff for roof beams. There are water channels carved to aid water collection. A small silo has been carved out of the solid rock on the south east extreme of the hill. A section of masonry on the west flank of the hill is of the type habitually built by Arab constructors of the 8th century onwards. The name Mezquita means mosque but the site seems more suited to defence than religion, but perhaps the Muslims were following the example of the Romans who are reputed to have sited a temple here. An excellent site too for Pagan sacrifice, in full view of all the Gods.

Retrace steps to the point where the rock ends and the meadow begins.

4. Immediately before the meadow a path crosses some slabs of rock on the right, then becomes clearer and joins a descending track after a few hundred metres.

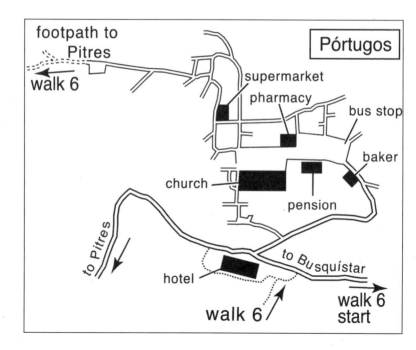

5. Turn right down the track. 30m after joining the track is a hairpin bend. This is the first of 5.

6. On the 5th hairpin on the deteriorating track take the path, left, heading north east. It is a clear established path following more or less on the contour to Busquístar 0.5km away.

   Busquístar has some pleasant corners to wander around but nothing special, over and above its position in the gorge and some of the best terraced land in a good state of maintenance. There are bars and a shop.

   If wanting to explore Busquístar any route will do, generally up, until meeting the main road at the top of the village. The express-way through the village is to turn left at the first houses and follow the roads that keep on the west edge of the village to meet the main road higher up.

7. Turn left along the main road. The road crosses the *barranco* by bridge and begins to rise. Later, ignore a concrete track on the right and two minor track branches on the left.

   After about 500m, on the bend in the road, a good track leaves the road left (2). Turn left down the track and 40m later branch right. The repeat of the route taken earlier to (3). Stay on the track until it branches right and left near its end, having passed the path to La Mezquita used earlier.

8. Take the path that continues a gently descending course between the two track branches. The path steepens and passes a house with landscaped garden. Keep right as passing the garden ignoring a left leading over to another house and eucalyptus tree.

   The path continues down steeply, passing another house on the immediate left. It zigzags left giving a good view of La Mezquita, then right.

9. Ignore a path joining from the left. Continue on the level path heading west. The path winds into a *barranco,* crosses it and climbs out.

   The path passes between two semi-ruinous buildings of a large mill and dwelling. The workings are visible by peering carefully over the left edge of the path. The horizontal paddle wheel at the lowest level is typical, although in earlier versions it would have been totally of wood. The stone-supported *acequia,* coming out of the *barranco* at a level higher than the building, brought water which would have been directed by stone channels down directly onto that horizontal paddle. The water jet came through a narrow orifice from a wide well structure integral with the buildings thereby multiplying its force. A vertical shaft rises from the paddle wheel to drive the machinery.

   This mill differs from any others in the area in having various relatively modern innovations. A pipe to take the water down to the wheel and a differential system that appears to be taking power to a belt drive. Unheard of sophistication in the normal low-tech design.

After the mill, follow the path to cross the *barranco* by bridge and a few minutes later arrive at a junction of paths, (10).

If looking for picnic spots, they don't come much better than the flat terraces just below the path on the exit from the *barranco* opposite the mill. Pórtugos is about 30 min away.

At the path junction the left option leads to Atalbéitar, a few hundred metres away. If not intending to do the complete walk, or Walk 7, then it is worth diverting to have a look.

10. Turn right at the path junction without crossing the bridge. Follow the path through a few hairpin bends and join a vague track. Turn left (north west) onto the track, which improves and forks.

11. Take the right fork, uphill.

12. After 100m where the track makes a hairpin to the right continue to the north on the path heading off the bend under the notable chestnut tree.

Nearing Pórtugos the path comes to the base of a high stone embankment. Turn right to join the main road. Turn left along the road to arrive at the hotel and start point.

Having arrived at Pórtugos the described walk is about half completed. It continues through the upper *barrío* of Pórtugos to pass later through Pitres, Mecina, Ferreirola and Atalbéitar. It returns to Pórtugos by repeating the last 15 minutes of walking described above.

13. From the hotel take the road into the village centre, signed "centro ciudad". Follow the village sketch plan(page 43) and after 30m turn left into a small street. Ignore an alley on the right, pass under the *tinao* to enter placeta San Sebastian, bear right.

At the T-junction go left and immediately right to enter the church square where the *fuente* provides good drinking water.

Take c. Cuatro Esquinas heading uphill. Continue into c. Eras at the cross roads. Fork left to arrive at the *fuente* and war memorial. Turn right into c. Rosario and follow it out of the village, ignoring left forks.

Fork right up to the cross (14) where c. Rosario broadens to a concrete road.

14. After the cross the route continues as a dirt road. At a fork, keep left. The track passes various houses on the left then divides around an old *cortijo*. Take the left fork.

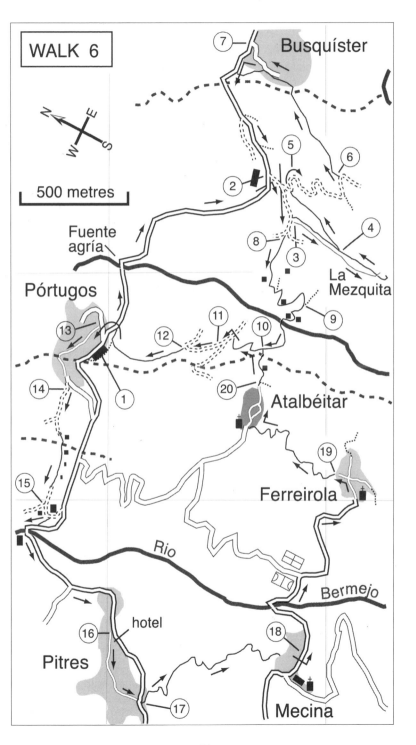

WALK 6

500 metres

Busquíster

Fuente
agría

Pórtugos

La
Mezquita

Atalbéitar

Ferreirola

Rio

Bermejo

hotel

Pitres

Mecina

15. Immediately after the fork the track bends round a large, newly constructed ham-drying building. Take the small path steeply down to the right, at the side of this building. Join the main road, turn right and follow it to Pitres.

16. On entering the village, just as the hotel comes into sight, fork right into the village. Pass through the *plaza* and out of it, downhill to meet the main road. See village plan page 55.

On joining the main road you will notice from the boats and anchors laid about that this is "The Port of Pitres". The boats bobbing about in El Puerto de Pitres are an a-political statement and a warning to us all about the nature of politics.

In the 19th century a visiting politician, anxious for votes, addressed the worthy citizens of Pitres: "Barbarians of Pitres, what can I give you?"

Barbarians, we assume, was a complimentary form of address referring to valour and ruthlessness in the battles of the 1568-71 Moorish rebellion. The complimentary nickname has stuck to this day for those born in Pitres.

The barbarians having heard all this before thought they might just as well test their candidate and be disappointed in a big way, as a small. They replied, "A sea port and two harvests each year".

"Agreed. They are yours," replied the politician, as they do.

To this day the society of fishermen of Pitres diligently work at cultivating crops of sardines on the terraces around the village. Coastal villages have made gifts of the boat and anchor so that they can be ready when, one day, a politician keeps his word.

17. Opposite the port a concrete road descends between the restaurant and the *ferretería*. Follow this round the back of the restaurant as it turns into a cobbled path. Ignore a minor path, right, at the end of the concrete section.

The main path continues clearly and steeply to arrive in Mecina, 200m vertically below, after about 15 minutes walk.

Mecina is apparently a maze of alleys but they all radiate like spokes from the era at the bottom of the path to meet the road below. Taking the leftmost spoke from the era leads to another example of the apparently strange things happening in The Alpujarra. El Atelier tea/reading rooms offer refreshment, intellectual stimulation and accommodation, a mixture sufficient for life. See village plan page 48.

18. On meeting the main road in Mecina, turn left (not past the hotel) and follow the road to Ferreirola, 15 minutes away. In Ferreirola pass the church and turn left at the wash-house.

19. The path leaves the village just on the uphill side of the *tinao*,

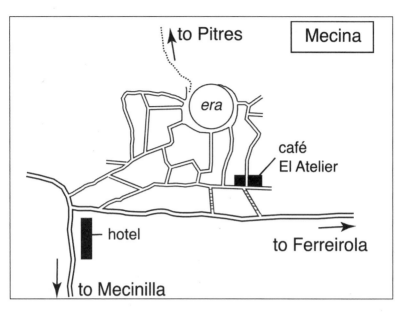

where the village street turns right and starts to descend to the B&B.

The path climbs all the way from Ferreirola up to Atalbéitar without difficulty, apart from the 150m of climb. At the road as it enters Atalbéitar turn right and any route leads to the village square and *fuente*. Another chance for rest and refreshment.

20. Leave the *plaza* of Atalbéitar by c. del Horno which soon fades to a path. Keep left at the cute, unmodernised wash-house. A few minutes later turn left, uphill at the path junction.

Follow the description from point (10) back to Pórtugos.

7. Six Villages of La Taha and the Gorge

Starting and finishing at Pitres the route covers the best of
La Taha, arrives at the bottom of the gorge but does not cross
the river. It can be done even in high summer, with an early
start or a long siesta at the river. Walk 9 is probably a better
version of this walk but is not suitable for very hot weather.
La Mezquita is included as a diversion for those who don't
intend to do Walk 6.

Time: 4 to 5 hours including rests and diversions. 8 hours if including a
mid-summer siesta.

Waymarks: Any waymarks passed are not of any significance.

Difficulties: The path on La Mezquita is a little awkward in some
places for the less agile. Between Atalbéitar and Ferreirola there is no
water. Take plenty, especially if you plan a long siesta at the river.

1. Start at the hotel on the main road, passing by Pitres. Turn left out
    of the hotel to follow the main road. 50m later take the first turn
    right, a village street which fades to a path almost immediately. (It
    may still be signed "Albergue" or youth hostel.)

2. Pass under an arch near the youth hostel. Immediately after the
    arch, turn right at the path junction and follow the *acequia*. After
    50m fork left, down away from the *acequia* into the valley of Río
    Bermejo with its ferrous waters.

3. Where the path joins a tarmac road, follow it downhill. Keep
    straight on at the next junction and follow the road into Atalbéitar.

*The water of the fuente in the square of Atalbéitar is the last
encountered for a good long while, best to fill up now.*

> Atalbéitar and other similar villages may be the hope of the future
> for The Alpujarra. Abandoned by all but half a dozen aged folk, it is
> now showing signs of repopulation by younger people who want to lead
> an alternative life style and work the small patches of land without
> expectation of putting money in the bank. This is the exact reverse of
> what happened a generation or two ago in these very villages.
>
> Explore all the alleys to the ultimate dead end, it is worth the few
> minutes spent. The critical eye will spot the best and worst of
> renovation techniques and, what has become, the famous rock of
> Atalbéitar. The size of a house, it demolished a few as it fell from the
> cliff above, during the wet years of 1994/5, and now sits there
> blocking one of the alleys.
>
> Leave the *plaza* by c. del Horno which soon fades to a path. Keep
> left at the cute unmodernised wash-house on the outskirts of the
> village.

4. A minute or two out of the village pass an isolated building on the

immediate right, then keep right at the path junction. A few hundred metres later, the path crosses a *barranco* by bridge and passes between the two buildings of a disused mill. (See description under Walk 6.) Just after the mill, cross another *barranco* and then fork left uphill where the path divides.

5. The path zigzags steeply up passing a house on the immediate right. It enters a clearing and bends left following the fence of a landscaped garden on the left. Continue to where the path joins a track and follow it.

6. Where the track reaches its highest point alongside a raspberry plantation and before passing a metal pylon, an *acequia* runs south along the hill shoulder between the two large flat meadows. This is the way to La Mezquita.

   At this point (6) the path to La Mezquita leaves the track. If you have not already visited this historic and beautiful site on Walk 6 you should do it now. Refer to Walk 6 points (3) to (5). Having followed those Notes you will be at point (8) on this walk, 7.

   Assuming that the diversion to La Mezquita is being omitted, continue on the track to where it joins another.

7. Turn right downhill.

8. On the first hairpin about 30m below, is a path to the right which can be used for access to La Mezquita.

9. On the 5th hairpin bend, including that at (8), take the path leaving to the right. A wire mesh fence begins to follow the right of the track just below this point.

   The path, an old mule track, heads off to the south west. Look for a left fork after a few hundred metres. It is 30m after some impressive rock overhangs where there is also a white concrete, pyramid-shaped boundary marker.

10. Take this minor path forking left and down, just as the main path curls to the right. The path drops down a very dry hill and the path, being of rock, on rock, is not obvious in some places. There are man-made stone edgings to the path all the way down to the river as it zigzags steeply down.

    There is a ruined mill at the river and a natural bridge giving access to some good shady resting places among the terraces. A path on the far side of the river heads upstream a few metres to a disused electricity generator, which is still there. Interestingly it used the same water supply system as the mill opposite; centuries old work for new-fangled purposes. New-fangled but defunct for 50 years.

    Take care near the river and please don't try to paddle.

11. From the mill the path heads north west without crossing the river.

It is easily followed to Ferreirola. There are a few turns to the right, all to be ignored.

There is a very special spring along the route just before reaching Ferreirola. It is easily recognised by its tiled surround, it is a champagne among waters and a beautiful, and cool place is provided for drinking it.

Ferreirola too is special; again it is worth exploring to the end of all its nooks and crannies. Like Fondales, Mecinilla, and the old quarters of Granada it is made more beautiful by the *carmenes* amongst the streets. All these places have been developed under the Muslims of the Middle Ages.

12. At the cross roads in Ferreirola, by the wash-house and *fuente*, take the downhill option. Keep right at the junction at the bottom, leaving c. Monteros on the left take the level street past the last few village houses. It should be signed GR142.

    A dirt path drops away south west from the village. Follow the zig-zags down, ignoring a right turn 30m from the last house. Cross a small, usually dry *barranco* by a bridge.

    The path drops again across some slabby, smooth rocks. Ignore a minor right turn here. The path continues clearly into the deep *barranco* of Río Bermejo and crosses by a concrete bridge. Later as the path begins to pass alongside a concrete *acequia* it approaches a magnificent chestnut tree.

13. At the tree continue going slightly down on the main path ignoring a right branch.It continues to drop slightly and at a T-junction of paths it turns right on the most used option.

    Just on the outskirts of Fondales the path crosses a *barranco* by a small bridge and continues straight on to pass under the *tinao* of the first house. At the *barranco* there are small left and right options to ignore. Map 9 (page 60) shows Fondales in some detail.

14. Turn right, up through the village to arrive at the nicely decorated *fuente* near the village car park.

    Fondales is very worthwhile exploring, see plan on map 9, before ending up at the *fuente* near the village car park at the village exit. If lacking energy for exploration the *fuente* with its charming decoration provides an ideal spot to recuperate and enjoy the sentiments. Each tile quotes a poem of love and lovers and their relation with the "village pump". Imagine a time when young girls were closely guarded by the family, but, she was almost certainly the one sent out to fetch the water. It would be a dim lad who didn't learn that the *fuente* was the place to snatch a moment with the girls.

    On the top, centre tile the *fuente* speaks to the girl:

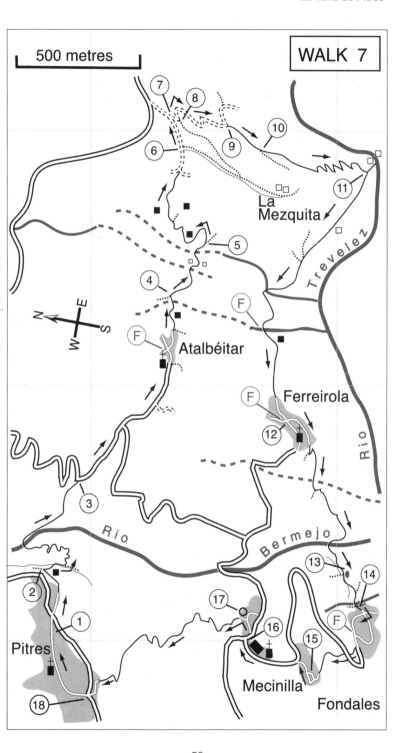

500 metres

WALK 7

La Mezquita

Trevelez

Atalbéitar

Ferreirola

Rio

Bermejo

Pitres

Mecinilla

Fondales

Fragile are hopes and dreams.
Like pitcher borne on hip,
Be strong in spring.
Oh! That your heart not suffer,
take from my fresh mouth,
the kisses not given by him.

The centre tile speaks of "The spring of dreams":

So many promises of love!
Scattered at your side,
embroidered, delicate,
with threads of silk!
So many carried by the wind.
So many to the altar, white as blossom.
So many to the convent.

Sitting here long enough I could happily cry to rival the *fuente*.

Leaving the *fuente*, pass the bus shelter with its fake chimney and take the next path on the right. It cuts a loop off the road and meets it again. The path crosses the road. It continues as a path opposite the row of garages. Follow the main path steeply up. It makes a sharp left bend at a tiny shed, water installation, and enters Mecinilla.

15. Turn right at the first junction of streets and follow on to the next where the *fuente* is. Turn right and the street can be followed to where it joins the car access road at Bar El Aljibe. A good place to rest before the last climb up to Pitres. Follow the road as it rises to pass the church.

16. Turn right just after the hotel and take the branch road sloping up left towards the houses.

There is a juxtaposition of old olive milling and pressing equipment at the road junction at Mecina but not in their intended positions (see illustrations page 39 and 75). The conical stones rolled in a circular path on a bed stone. More nice ceramics too. These here liken the three villages of Mecina, Mecinilla and Fondales to three pretty little girls with Moorish eyes, little drums and slippers of silver and gold. Three Arab princes in far off lands languish on not being able to breathe these airs nor drink the waters full of Alpujarran sky, life and soul.

Tea and culture are available in the Café Atelier, see sketch map page 48.

Any route uphill through the village streets of Mecina will lead to the *era*.

17. The path to Pitres leaves from the top left of the *era*. 30 minutes of slow plodding along the obvious path leads to the main road at Pitres (18).

8. A Short Stroll above Pitres

Time: 1½ to 3 hours depending on capacity to dawdle

Waymarks: Only the red/white GR7 marks are useful. The route follows the GR7 from point (8) to Pitres.

1. Start from the village square of Pitres and walk up past the church and pharmacy.

2. Using the sketch of Pitres village find a path leaving the north corner of the village. It is a dirt path heading slightly up from the last house where the village street turns downhill.

3. After a few minutes walk join a tarmac road and turn left. Pass one set of hairpin bends. At the next sharp bend, where the sign board for Capilerilla village is, a track branches right on the bend.

4. Turn right onto the track. 20m later, fork right ignoring the steeply climbing left branch. Pass various goat corrals and two branch tracks to the left. Pass a newly constructed stone house on the right.

5. Just as passing a second new stone house, look for a path rising steeply to the left into the trees. It branches immediately, keep right.

   There are a number of minor turns but the main path is clear. Early on in the climb a minor right path leads onto a rocky promontory giving clear views east across the gorge of Río Bermejo. Later when nearly out of the chestnuts there is a gaily-painted house on the immediate left of the path.

6. The path crosses an *acequia* then joins the well-made forestry track. Turn left onto the track. The track is followed for about 2km. At first it is accompanied by an *acequia* on its left. It passes a large round water storage building (7).

   A wire mesh fence begins to run along the left of the track. Continue on the track to where it is joined by another rising from the left.

8. Turn hairpin left onto the track at the junction. From this point on, the route coincides with the GR7 to Pitres.

9. About 0.5km later is another track junction. Turn right. 20m later take the path left, at the point where a chain usually blocks the track.

   About 200m later the path is joined by others from the right and left in an area where there are some old metal fence posts. Follow the posts keeping them on the right. The path drops steeply past a ruin and *era*.

10. Just below the *era*, cross an *acequia* and follow the path as it turns to the left, crosses a small stream and leads obviously on to Capilerilla to the east.

11. 100m before Capilerilla is the village wash-house then a T-junction of paths. Keep left.

12. At the first village street, turn right and immediately left along the street with three *tinaos*.

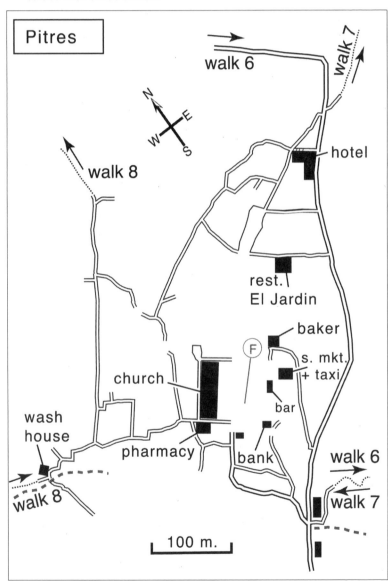

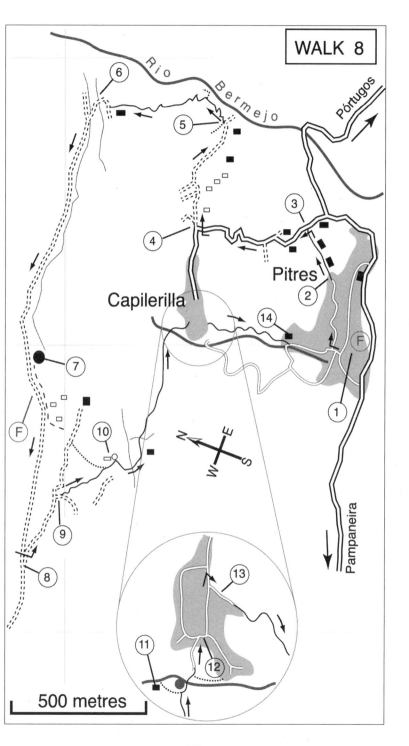

La Taha de Pitres

WALK 8

500 metres

13. Take the first right turn after the *tinaos*. This concrete street descends and soon becomes a cobbled path leading clearly down to Pitres.

14. Keep left at the wash-house on entering Pitres. Continuing downhill will lead back to the start point.

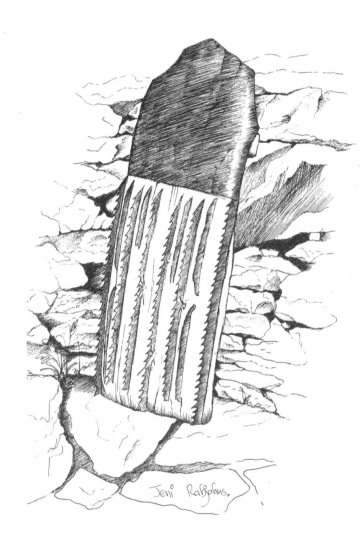

Threshing sledge

9. The Best Alpujarran Path

If time only permits you one walk in the Taha, then this should be the one. It includes the lower villages, starting at Mecina, crosses to the other side of the Río Trevelez where it uses the best path in The Alpujarra. Once on the far side, looking at the Sierra Nevada from that different aspect is interesting and the complete Taha with its nine villages will be laid out before you. The map for Walk 6 will enable this walk to be joined from any of the villages not included.

Time: 4 hours walking but better treated as an all day walk, with picnic and diversions 6 hours or more.

Difficulties: not good in the summer, it's too hot once the river is crossed.

1. Start at the hotel in Mecina. Turn left out of the hotel, pass the church to arrive at the Bar *Aljibe* of Mecinilla. Take the village road to the right of El *Aljibe*.

   At the *fuente* turn left and later take the left turn leading under the *tinao* to the edge of the village. The path from the bottom of Mecinilla joins the road.

2. Cross the road and take the path to the immediate right of the row of garages. On meeting the road again turn left into Fondales, and keeping to the left pass the *fuente* (3).

   Walk 7 Notes also mention this *fuente* but since we are here I can't resist quoting to you the rhyme on the bottom tile:

   > To the little Isabel
   > She had dirt on face,
   > and hair like dead grass,
   > some beautiful eyes
   > with the shine of spring

3. Fill up with water here or at the *fuente* at the bottom of the village by the wash-house (4).

It will be a few hours before passing more water.

4. At the wash-house the track turns to the right and 20m later steeply down left. Where the cobbles end, it turns to the right and continues as a small path. It zigzags at first then angles down towards poplar and chestnut trees on its way to the "Roman" bridge by the ruined mill (5).

   This incarnation of the bridge may or may not be Roman but I trust it more than the 20th century railings. The best view of it is from the chestnut trees a few hundred metres before. This almost certainly would have been a Roman route. They are known to have had a town at Torvizcón to the south, a port at Almuñecar, the temple on La Mezquita and all accessible by this route. Rome too presumably.

The path up the hill, or cliff, on the far side of the bridge is one of the most special features of The Alpujarra. An engineering feat, a beautiful piece of work on which nature in its different seasons works its own magic. Take lots of time over the climb, stop and stare at every opportunity. Imagine yourself as a 1,000-year-old mule and sit down a lot, stubbornly.

5. It takes about an hour to plod up the hill having crossed the bridge, and to arrive at the junction with the track (6).

    The described route turns left at (6). There is however, quite an interesting diversion to the right which takes half an hour or so and could be a good picnic spot. Turning right and keeping right at any junctions leads to La Loma de Algibe. Here there is an Arabic *aljibe* in almost perfect state of preservation. A domed water store which even now sometimes fills when rains fall or springs become active. The importance of this building in the middle of nowhere was as a service station on this 1,000-year-old "M1".

    The turn to the right here leads down to some civil war bunkers so maybe even then it was thought an important route.

6. Having turned left along the track no great effort is required in a route finding sense. About 4km later, at a group of houses, take the branch track descending to the left (7).

    On a hot day if looking for a picnic spot with shade the choice is either amongst the pines which extend for about half the distance along the track or at point (9) which offers views, water, sun or shade.

    At around point (7), by getting on some high ground it is possible to look over south east into the valley of the Río Guadalfeo which is of interest if you haven't visited that area yet. (see chapter – miscellaneous walks).

7. Take the branch track left and follow it down to a rocky promontory making a natural viewing platform (9).

    The ruins (8) at the right of the track are of Los Baños de Panjuila, frequented for medicinal bathing until the 20th century. Some sources believe that this site was a Hammam since Arabic times, providing public baths on this 1,000-year-old "motorway" linking La Taha to the port of Adra.

9. Water is available to the left of the track where a stream flows, just below the visible wall and gate. Shady siesta spots too, amongst the poplars.

    The path continues from the end of the track down another

La Taha de Pitres

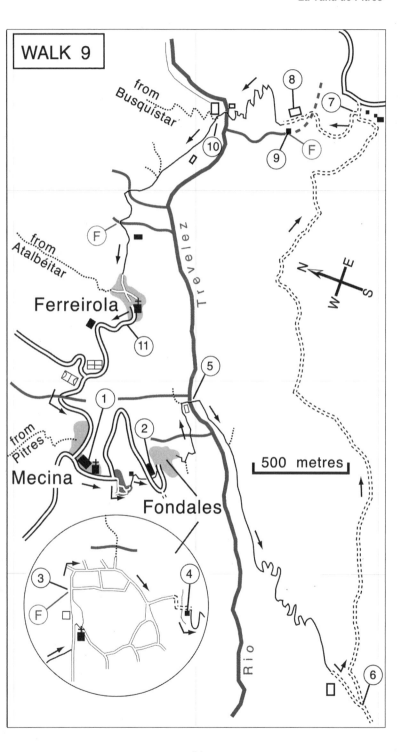

WALK 9

from Busquistar

from Atalbéitar

from Pitres

Ferreirola

Mecina

Fondales

Trevelez

Rio

500 metres

N E W S

impressive path with good views up the river valley towards Trevelez.

On the way down there are good birds-eye views of the mill ruins. The path-like line leading to it, parallel to the river is its *acequia* bringing water to the two well-like water chambers behind the building. These two chambers would have provided the head of water to drive the two stones or more likely one or the other, one stone being finer the other courser, for different grains – wheat, oats and maize being the most common.

10. On leaving the mill take the most obvious path. It heads up across the hill, west, and leads obviously on to Ferreirola. There are one or two right turns to ignore.

It is worth tasting the water from the fuente, decorated with tiles. These nicely illustrate the cycle of vine culture, wine production and use, all under the control of sun and moon. Almost all facets of traditional life in The Alpujarra are controlled by the relevant phase of the correct moon.

11. From Ferreirola the route returns to Mecina by following the main road out of the village past the church.

If needing to return to Pitres or Pórtugos follow map 6 to Atalbéitar and Pórtugos or the reverse of map 7, Atalbéitar – Pitres.

Panniers of esparto on mule

Trevelez

Factfile: Trevelez

Buses: It is on the Granada – Alcutar route, see Appendix A.

Accommodation: of all types, see Appendix B

Shops: It is hard to find anything other than knick-knack shops and ham at the main road level, but normal shops exist in *barrío medio*

Bank: near the church in Plaza Iglesia

Medical Emergency: nearest 24hr centre is in Pitres.

Most interesting fiesta: in honour of the 'Virgin of the snows' the village organises a *romeria* in early August. The virgin is carried to the peak of Mulhacén where there is a shrine. This involves a long walk and a night out on the mountain for the faithful.

Restaurants: A wide choice, from the famous La Fragua to a hundred humbler bars in the upper barrios. You'll probably be thrown out if you don't order ham but try also for trout which should be fresh from the Río Trevelez, but....

Trevelez is a village with a one-track mind: *Jamón Serrano*. The guide-books and publicity slice the romance of air-cured ham hanging in caves rather thickly. The reality is that the village is disappearing behind a wall of huge ham-curing warehouses and one has to be quite determined to break through its defences on the main road to find the charm above. The ham is good and the business is good; if only the neo-ham architecture was a little less obtrusive everyone would be happy, except perhaps the pigs . Neon hams on the top of buildings, one feels are a bit too tasteless.

From the walker's point of view, Trevelez has interest through its position as the highest village in The Alpujarra (and in Spain), by sitting in a beautiful valley and by being the nearest access point to *the* place to visit in the Sierra Nevada, *Las Siete Lagunas*. The village itself is charming. The lower and middle barrios are now hard to separate but each is centred on its *plaza*. The upper barrio remains a little isolated physically and in character. No one expects tourists to walk that far, so it has remained less developed and worth a visit for that reason.

The lie of the land at Trevelez makes finding shorter, easier walks difficult but even if you can't manage the long walks, the village is worth a visit. It can take half a day to amble round the three barrios, taking the occasional coffee or *vino costa* with tapa (of ham, one presumes). Following the town plan sketch you can find a track heading down to the river and spend a very pleasant time walking up-river on the West bank as far as you wish; i.e. the reverse of Walk 10. The river valley path also makes a relatively easy access to the Sierra Nevada ridge. Expeditionists wishing to walk the Sierra Nevada ridge eastwards to Puerto de la Ragua could use this route.

If the walk to the *Siete Lagunas* is beyond you and you are the horse riding type then you might like to go on horseback. Ask at Hotel La Fragua or in Barrío Alto "Rutas a Caballo" 958 858601.

10. The Río Trevelez and the Río Culo de Perro

A really scenic walk with lots of water and greenery. It passes by some real *cortijos* in the sense of being working farms, inhabited most of the year. It is probably a better summer walk than winter one because of the amount of water about. With waterproof boots the winter would not be a problem. There is a clearly visible path throughout. In hot weather point (10) is a good target to have in mind for lunch and siesta.

Time: 6 hours. 8 hours including riverside siesta.

Difficulties: the bridge at point (7) is not to everyone's taste. It may not be safe for those whose balance is not good. Paddling the river here is possible usually, but in rapid thaw situations the force of the water is too much for safety. The sketch map indicates a higher route for those who don't like the look of the crossing or bridge.

---

1. From the main through road head up through the village streets, start with c. Real. Keep taking uphill options to pass the wash-house and arrive at Plaza Iglesia and the church of the lower *barrio*.

   Take c. *Cuesta*, aptly named, which leads up through the flower-bedecked c. Pereza to, at last a level street, c. Carcel. Turn right along c. Carcel then hairpin left to pass Hotel La Fragua. Passing through the arch after the hotel leads up to the wash-house in c. Horno.

   Turn right and follow the deteriorating street to where it levels and a cobbled path (2) heads off at right-angles to the street, opposite the front door of a house.

2. Take the cobbled path off c. Horno.

   Calle Carcel leading from Plaza Barrio Medio to the bar La Fragua is the hub of the middle of the three barrios of Trevelez. I always seem to delay my Trevelez walks by taking a last minute coffee in this area and also fall gratefully into one of its bars on returning. If you are thinking along these lines, nip into the Panaderia Federico near the plaza. Something from their excellent selection of pastries and sweets, would go well with the coffee or supplement the picnic. I particularly recommend the dulces de coco y almendras, ("dulthez de koko ee almendras") macaroon type cakes with coconut, which are just the things to find in a rucsac to re-animate flagging folk near the end of a walk.

   Bar La Fragua is well known as the place for gourmet dining in The Alpujarra. Avoid weekends, particularly Sunday lunchtime when they seem to be overrun.

The path soon crosses an *acequia* by bridge, and continues climbing on the far side. It zigzags up alongside a Poplar filled *bco.*, crosses it, then passes immediately to the left of a *cortijo*. Ignore a minor hairpin left. Continue on the clear path into a second poplar-filled *barranco* passing to the right of a *cortijo*, ignoring a left fork, to cross the water. Zigzag up between an *era* and a ruin with Walnut trees. More zigzags pass to the right of a *casa de campo*.

3. Note the path passing between two buildings of a stone *cortijo*. A two-storey building to the left and single-storey corral to the right.

4. Ignore a left turn which normally has a variety of Waymarks. This leads up towards *Las Siete Lagunas* a longer walk for another day (see Walk 11).

The path heads obviously on, climbing only very gradually, heading for a flatter broad ledge (5) between the upper and lower crags of *Crestones* de los Posteros.

The path zigzags up to cross the shoulder of the hill and continue on, now with a view of the *Río Culo de Perro* valley, down gradually towards the river.

6. At the forking of paths take the right fork on a lower route to the bridge.

7. Bridge or paddle that is the question.

If paddling, be sure the water is not too forceful for you and keep the boots on. take the socks off by all means. If the crossing looks dangerous go back to (6) and take the higher route, marked on the sketch map.

On the far side of the bridge the path passes up through a soggy area, SE, to a large *cortijo* and a grand *era*.

On the way up between (7) and (8) off to the left look for a grove of huge cherry trees. They provide a pleasant oasis for rest and shade if required. Just behind and above them is an earth *alberca* fed by a spring. This is the last shade until reaching (10) so it's worth taking advantage of it and freshening the water bottles.

The *era* behind the *cortijo* is, as they all seem to be, something special. This one must get nearly top marks for its beautiful stone work, polished and shiny from use. Its position too seems to have been thought out as a viewpoint rather than a winnowing site. Looking up the *Río Culo de Perro* in summer gives a view of a huge bowl of country from the foreground on the right covered with Oak, lower down the Cherry grove, past a multitude of dividing *barrancos*, up higher to massive slopes covered in a green blush of grass.

The grass is thanks to the care given to the *acequias de careo* by the owner of the *era* on which you stand. This gentleman has lived in this rather way out spot all his life; when asked if it wasn't

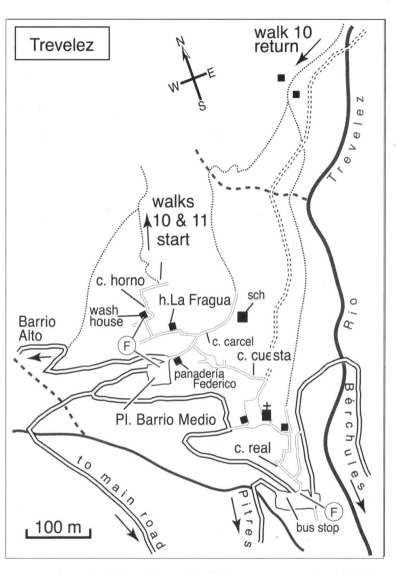

sometimes a little lonely he replied "No, I have 400 cows" which is the
sort of intriguing answer one gets from asking silly questions. In
summer he cares for the hills which feed his cattle, in winter he takes
them to the milder *sierras* of Córdoba. This journey he used to do on
foot with all the cattle, along the *veredas* that networked the
country. Stopping in *posadas* where possible, the journey would take
him about a month.

In June he would make the return trip to the *cortijo*, here in the
Sierra Nevada. He still follows this way of life but the cattle travel by

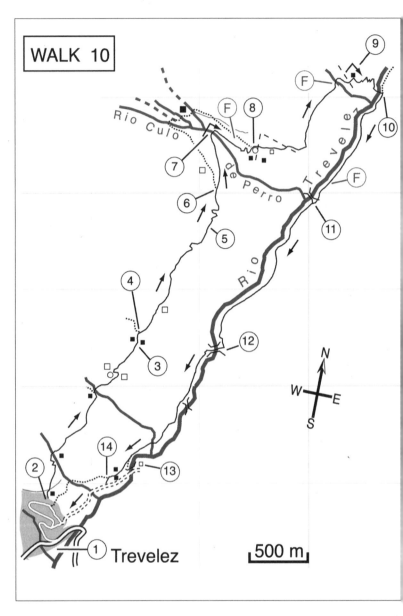

WALK 10

Rio Culo

de Perro

Rio Trevele

Trevelez

500 m

N
W — E
S

lorry along motorways that have cut the *veredas* and made them unusable. He seems happy to adapt an old way of life to modern conditions.

8. From the *era* the path leads off through the fence eastwards. It passes immediately to the left of a ruin a few hundred metres from the *era* and continues angling uphill north east to pass through a fence and turn right.

We now begin to lose sight of the Culo de Perro valley but before rounding the shoulder of the hill there is the possibility of absorbing three splendid views up and down the two valleys that join somewhat below.

The path continues, gradually down, after rounding the shoulder. It aims towards a *cortijo* visible ahead at (9), about 1 km ahead on the far side of a *barranco*. After crossing the *barranco* (more good drinking water) the path is a little difficult. It crosses the small *acequia* and zigzags a little below it, before passing through a fence and coming in sight of the *cortijo*.

9.   The path does a hairpin right opposite the front door of the *cortijo* and zigzags steeply down to the river. It turns right along the upper side of a wire fence for about 100m to arrive at the bridge (10).

The route back to Trevelez is now all along the river in the downstream direction but if it's time for lunch or a siesta it might be better to go upstream for 5 or 10 minutes to take advantage of some good shade and relatively dry places to sit. Trevelez is at least 2 hours walk from this point.

10. Turn right and follow the path downstream on the east bank.

11. Ignore a bridge crossing to the west, where the *Culo de Perro* valley joins.

12. Follow the path over the bridge to the west side. The path now remains on the west bank all the way.

Passing through the water meadows here is a pleasure. Lots of wetland plants to find and possibly the cattle and their music to admire. Yes they have big horns but they are cows and placid. Try not to frighten them or separate cow from calf. When passing though any wire gates please leave them as you found them. Fences come and go as temporary measures as cattle are moved from area to area.

Nearing the village the path comes in sight of Peñabon and Piedra Ventana, the crags to the south-east and then a new-looking goat corral on the opposite bank (13).

Soon after noting the goat corral the path passes between two houses about 30m off the path. The path forks (14). The quickest and easiest route to the nearest bar is to go left, join the track and follow it to the village. The right fork climbs to enter the village in the *barrio medio* near Bar La Fragua.

11. Las Siete Lagunas – 3000m

The walk is to *the* special place of the Sierra Nevada. It is a walk for late spring and summer as soon as the snows have retreated to about 3000m. It is a strenuous walk and to give the maximum amount of time at the *lagunas* the **Notes** assume the same route up and down. Younger, stronger, fitter walkers will be able to include an ascent of Mulhacén for which they should allow an extra 3 hours.

Time: 7½ to 10 hours for the return trip. The ideal is to allow 4 hours for the ascent, 4 hours for the descent and 4 hours for rest and exploration of the *lagunas*. The *lagunas* are spread over an area of a square kilometre, and the difference in height between the highest and lowest is about 100m.

Waymarks: The route is waymarked with yellow/white banded wooden posts. These are very widely spaced and not to be relied on. The path is well trodden and visible except in snow.

Difficulties: The route climbs to a height of 3000m (10,000ft). It climbs 1500m (5,000ft) in about 9 km. Then the descent in reverse.

If unsure of your fitness for this amount of climbing don't attempt it. The temperatures at the lagunas will be 10ºC less than at the village, simply by virtue of the altitude. At this height people with breathing problems (e.g. asthma) find them greatly exacerbated. Choose a day in a stable period of weather but be prepared for bad weather and strong winds. Observe the normal safety and survival rules.

---

1. Using the town plan; leave the village by c. Horno. To ease the initial steep climb through the village, parking is possible in Plaza Iglesia and higher up in Plaza Barrio Medio.

    Walking up c. Horno from the wash-house the road deteriorates, does a right angle bend and passes a few houses before continuing out of the village on the contour.

2. The path branches off c. Horno opposite the front door of a house on the flat stretch. It is a cobbled path climbing steeply.

    Walks 10 and 11 coincide between points (2) and (4) and more detail is given under Walk 10.

3. About 2.5km after leaving the village note the path passing between the two buildings of a *cortijo*. A stone-built two-storey building on the left and single-storey corral to the right.

4. 50m past point (3) is a division of paths; take the left. The junction is usually well marked with waymarks of one sort or another and there is also a huge boulder on the right whose shape seems to point the way left.

The path zigzags to a fence about 50m from (4).

Pass through the fence and continue on a clear path past a square, wire-fenced enclosure on the right.

5. The most obvious path then bends left, south. Follow it, ignoring some less obvious right turns. After a few zigzags the clear path bends round to north west, following the general line of a wire strand fence climbing the hill.

Just before meeting *Acequia Gorda* the path bends round to the north, levels out, passes through a wire strand fence and gradually climbs to meet the *acequia*. The path continues along the upper side of the *acequia* for about 50m then passes through a wire mesh fence into an area of young struggling conifers.

The path heads generally north aiming at a rocky outcrop on the skyline but first it zigzags up the side of a gully running on about 290°. The path levels for a while continuing its northward route to another rock outcrop on the shoulder of the hill; then resuming its relentless zigzag climb through struggling pines.

About now the view ahead opens out and we start to see our target to the north west: the waterfalls pouring out of *Las Siete Lagunas* in their as-yet invisible hanging valley.

7. Leave the area of pines through the mesh fence and follow the continuing path to Acequia del Mingo 50m ahead.

Cross the *acequia* using the path tending right which immediately leaves the *acequia* to cross the *Prado Largo* with its ruin, *era* and stone corral.

The path now passes through the sort of country that pumps pure joy into the blood, probably doing lasting damage to the brain. In summer, rivulets of sparkling water, form and flow through the flatter meadow areas of deeper soil, bright green with healthy growth and dotted with treasures. I like to lie down on this oozing green sponge, take a last wary look around for predators and drink from the flow of new water. The romance of the occasion often dispelled by the contents of my open rucksack falling out, over my head into the water.

These damp summer pastures are known as *borreguiles*, literally meaning sheep pastures; they have great significance to shepherds who traditionally move their flocks higher and higher as the year progresses, following the grass.

The path follows the line of *Acequia* del Mingo but at slightly greater altitude. It crosses two or three small tributaries before coming down to *Río Culo de Perro* just upstream of a concrete dam-like structure (8).

Ahead are four waterfalls (depending on conditions and

71

season), a pair to the left (280º) and a pair to the right. (Another fall marked on the sketch map is downstream and out of sight). A cliff and scree separate the two pairs. The route aims for the right most pair. In snow and ice-free conditions there is no problem in zigzagging up between the two falls of the right most pair. In other conditions take the diversion indicated on the sketch map.

8. Cross the river and follow the path on about 320° to the confluence of waters at the bottom of the falls.

9. Cross to between the two falls and looking carefully for the zigzags it is not too difficult to walk up.

If daunted by the prospect, bear in mind the diversion mentioned above which is marked on the sketch map as a descent route. In good conditions there is no scrambling involved.

10. Wow!

    With luck the weather will be kind to you and you will be comfortable here for a few hours. Please explore as much as you have energy for and I wish you everything *Las Siete Lagunas* have given me. To the east of Laguna Hondera is a metal post box of the mountaineering society. South from here on the other side of the water 50m away among the rocks, is a natural refuge if needing shelter from weather. Also in that direction is the start of a route up the scree for those who want to continue on to Mulhacén's peak. Allow 3 hours for the return trip.

Descent to Trevelez

The quickest way back is to follow the ascent route in reverse. Described below is a slight variation for those who would like to avoid the steep descent down the falls. It rejoins the outward route at *Prado Largo* (7).

11. From the metal mountaineers post box near Laguna Hondera pick up the path heading east to cross the stream above the more easterly waterfall.

    Passing eastwards around the top of the cliffs gives a view of the ascent route from the dark patch of conifers the path and *acequia* leading up from *Prado Largo* (7).

    0.5km below the path is an *acequia* leaving the falls and heading east. It may look more like a path from above when it is empty.

12. On arriving at a line of craggy rocks the path, which is marked with red paint, makes a hairpin turn to the right and zigzags down the shoulder of the hill in a south east direction to meet the *acequia* below.

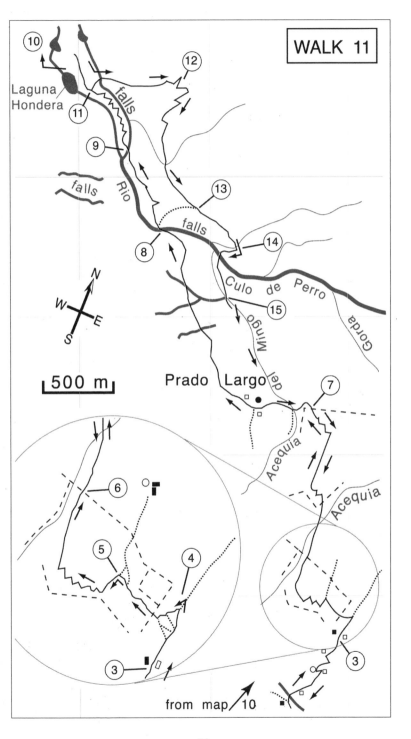

WALK 11

10

Laguna
Hondera

11

falls

falls

Rio

9

12

13

14

8

N
W   E
S

500 m

Culo de Perro

del Mingo

15

Gorda

Prado Largo

7

Acequia

6

Acequia

5

4

3

3

from map 10

73

Cross the *acequia* and continue down the shoulder following red paint marks.

13. The path which is easiest underfoot turns to the right, west, to find its way to the concrete dam structure in the river bed at (8) from where it is possible to retrace the upward route, to Prado Largo (7).

If following the direct descent from (8) to (7) make sure to follow the path that crosses Prado Largo and keeps left to pass corral, *era* ruin and then cross the *acequia* to (7). *Ignore a good path which branches right and stays above the Acequia del Mingo.*

If visibility is bad and the concrete dam cannot be seen it is probably better to continue down the shoulder to point (14). Although there is no visible path, by staying on the high ground of the shoulder until reaching the acequia below, the position is fixed.

For the sake of variety and to get a sight of the falls downstream from (8), and an increasingly good view of the *Río Culo de Perro* I describe the route below. It passes (14) and joins Acequia del Mingo leading to Prado Largo (7).

After the red paint marked path has diverged from the shoulder there is no visible path. Continue on the high ground of the shoulder, neither losing height to left or right.

14. Arrive at the point where the *acequia* bends around the shoulder. Cross the *acequia* and follow it back towards the river 150m to the West.

15. A path crosses the river just below the exit of Acequia del Mingo and climbs gradually to meet and cross it. Once on the upper bank of Acequia del Mingo there is an easy and defined path back to *Prado Largo*. Take care not to walk past *Prado Largo* which is at a slightly higher level than the *acequia* and not visible from it.

Watch out for the mesh fence (7) and the area of pines. Follow the path descending from the *acequia* to pass through the fence at (7).

7. The route is now the same as that used to ascend and is well defined all the way back to Trevelez.

The *acequia* passed between (12) and (13) and that at (14) show well a system of water management known as *Acequias de Careo*. These acequias are not designed to carry water anywhere in particular but to distribute it gently across the hillside. Having an exit every 20m or so the water escapes to irrigate the hillside and by filtration enters natural underground systems which, it has been shown, spring forth again at much lower levels, three months later, to be reused by villagers and irrigators. A vast natural reservoir therefore exists with

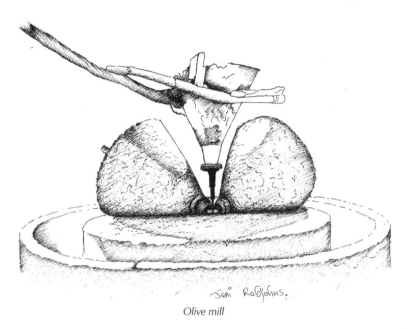

Olive mill

an ecological value; as opposed to the modern solutions of pipes and concrete dams which have hidden costs.

These high level *acequias* cannot be attributed to the industry of the Moors but to those who succeeded them in the 16th century. The Moors confined themselves to lower altitudes nearer the villages. The re-populants from other areas of Spain, with their background as cereal growers, found the higher ground more suitable for that purpose and increased land use into the peaks. The word *careo* is local to Salamanca and means pasture, an interesting indication of how culture, people, industry and language must have changed at that time.

Bérchules

Fact File

Buses: Bérchules is the only village served by a bus service to Almería. It is also on the Granada route like the other villages (see Appendix A).

Accommodation: of various levels from hotel to self-catering (see Appendix B)

Shops: Supermarkets, corner shops, Post office

Bank: Yes, nearest cashpoint in Cadiar

Medical Emergency: Pharmacy in Plaza de Abastos. 24 hour emergency in Cadiar (15 minutes by car); Doctor's surgery next to town hall.

Restaurants: Hotel Bérchules and Bar Triana at entrance to village, under the town hall. Bars in each of the *plazas.*

Bérchules is off the beaten track as far as most visitors to The Alpujarra are concerned. It is well worth a visit if for no other reason than to take advantage of its very pleasant hotel, which serves as a good base for exploring all the area East of Trevelez dealt with in this guide. The village itself is just off the main road, which enhances its remote feel. It is normally a quiet sleepy place but like all the villages it becomes packed to the last bunk bed in July/August and at the other main *fiesta* times (see Appendix B).

Apart from the walks specified below it is pleasant to meander the streets and alleys of the village above the church and it is possible to walk down the road which leaves the car park (see town plan) to a picnic spot in the river bed. A health giving spring at the picnic spot may be just what we all need.

Anyone of a perverse nature may like to time their visit for July and celebrate New Years Eve on 31st with the rest of the village. Practise eating a grape for each of the 12 bongs of midnight; an essential *Noche Vieja* activity.

Jeni Rabjohns. '01

12. A long half-day from Bérchules

A half-day walk whose main interests are a beautifully made stone *acequia*, an equally impressive stone-laid mule path, ascending a valley side which one would think to defy paths, and a panoramic view of the region.

Time: 4 to 5 hours.

Waymarks: The first part of the route follows the GR7/E4 towards Mecina Bombarón and a sign on the edge of the village points the way. Red/white paint marks and wooden posts about 40cm in height will be encountered but the route diverges away from these at point (4).

Difficulties: No real problems except quite a lot of height gain and loss for a relatively short walk. No water encountered.

1. Start from the Fuente de las Carmelitas near the town hall and head into the village. See village plan page 79.

   The inscription on the fuente alludes to a Carmelite parish priest who, ignoring the water's special properties, drank and "in an instant" found himself in love and married. The wording warns or advises that any of us drinking here can 'suffer' the same fate. So fill your bottles and let's get on with it, it's your last chance.

   Follow c. Iglesia (not c. Baja Iglesia) to arrive at the church in Plaza Obispo Miguel Peinado. Pass the church and take the uphill option to Plaza de Abastos where the bar Vaquero and pharmacy can be found.

   Leave Plaza de Abastos by c. Real, turn right into c. Aqua and follow it, through a mini-plaza with fountain, to its end, ignoring any rights and lefts. At the end of c. Aqua is a wooden GR7/E4 sign-post, (possibly hidden under a huge growth of fig) pointing down the path. It zigzags down and crosses a small *barranco* with water flowing, passing between large walnut and chestnut trees. Later, passing an *era* and *casa de campo*, ignore a path hairpin right.

   The route follows the major path crossing two more small water flows, heading up the valley and always angling downhill to arrive at a ruined mill and a bridge across the river. Over the bridge, turn right and follow the stone-laid path.

   It's a tough climb up, but on a beautiful path which cleverly gets up the cliff with the minimum of gradient. On some of the lower, smooth rocky sections step like indentations, the size and shape of mule hooves, have been worn in by passing generations, following foot for foot. A slow steady progress up brings one to a grassy promontory with an impressive era and good views to enjoy while getting the breath back.

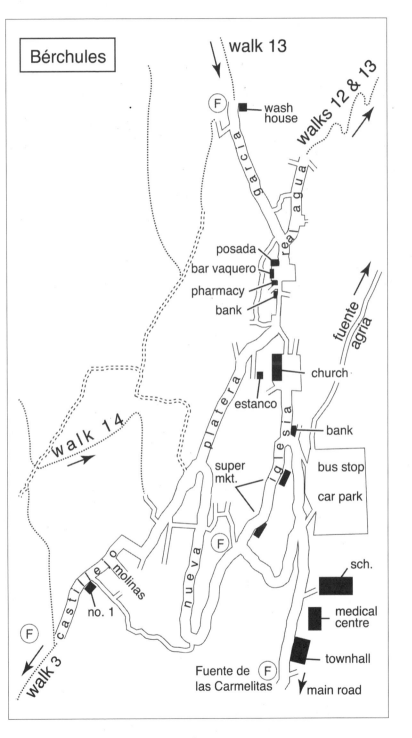

Bérchules

walk 13

F

wash
house

walks 12 & 13

garcia

real agua

posada

bar vaquero

pharmacy

bank

fuente agria

church

estanco

platera

bank

walk 14

super
mkt.

iglesia

bus stop

car park

F

nueva

sch.

molinas

castillo

no. 1

medical
centre

F

walk 3

Fuente de
las Carmelitas

F

townhall

main road

2. From the *era* the route turns left and follows the left-hand side of a broken wall until meeting with a wire mesh fence. Turn right to keep the fence on the left. The path crosses an almost level area, diverging away from the fence to follow some terrace edges looking like metre high earth embankments.

Pass in front of a small stone ruin and then onto the stone-built terrace edge ahead. The track, visible as a horizontal line above, is the next target to aim for.

There are various paths leading up to it but that of easiest gradient is the best choice, joining the track just before it heads around into the next valley.

The point where you join the track is an hour or more from the start. Before turning your back temporarily on Bérchules and its valley, it is a good place to have breakfast and enjoy the rest.

The name 'Las Bérchules' we are told is derived from the plural of the word *vergel* which in the Spanish pronunciation sounds very similar. It means a verdant garden filled with flowers; the surrounding terraces do always seem to be green, even in summer there is enough grazing to keep the cattle fed and they, incidentally always provide a musical background with their bongling bells. The ladies of the village keep up the flowery image by festooning their houses with flowering potted plants, some of them to an extreme extent.

The river at this point is named Río Grande de Las Bérchules but it is in effect the Río Guadalfeo, the dominant river of the Alpujarra. From this point westwards it collects all the rivers draining from the Sierra Nevada and passes out to the sea near Motril. It will, we assume, fill the reservoir being constructed at Rules, a few kilometres from the coast.

Looking down the valley, Cádiar, regarded as being at the head of the Guadalfeo, can be seen sitting in the bottom of an already ample valley. Looking upstream the route followed from the era can be seen and gives a good impression of the depth of the gorge it managed to cross. Further upstream still, the cliffs get higher and the gorge deeper and this area can be seen by following Walk 13. Nearer the skyline on the highest ground, patches of snow normally remain throughout the year, feeding the river.

3. Turn right along the track and follow it to a junction about 1km on. Ignore the hairpin left but look for an indistinct track 30m further, on the left.

4. Follow this track (which diverged right off a newly bulldozed track going straight up the hill) across the hill to a vineyard 100 metres or so away surrounded by a wire mesh fence.

Vines for wine production are not let to grow into vines but are pruned back to the stump, annually each winter. The Spanish sensibly have two (at least) different words for 'vine vines' and 'stump vines' thereby avoiding confusing themselves in the way I confuse you.

This vineyard and a few others like it must be, at 1400m, the highest in Europe – it works, I have drunk from this very vineyard. The wine produced is a dry, strongly alcoholic, rosado, which ages to a brown colour. It always had a sherry-ish flavour and is best drunk young when it still had its fresh pink colour and flavour of fruit. It is, for most people new to the area, an acquired taste but it's worth a try. Order "vino costa", it may come out of a dodgey looking plastic bottle under the counter but so much the better, it means the landlord probably made it himself and it has not been through all those nasty clean stainless steel tubes in the factory. Anyway it has enough alcohol content to kill anything; if you want to walk tomorrow two glasses are probably enough.

Follow the fence of the vineyard uphill until it turns away to the right. The route continues uphill towards the track above. The route now is following the vereda marked on the IGN maps as a broad double dotted line. There is usually nothing visible on the ground of these drove routes but here, just ahead is a short section bordered by double ruined walls which leads to the modern track and disappears.

The point at which the vereda joins the track is marked by a pair of holly oaks and from this point a few more scattered oaks are visible uphill, West on the other side of the track.

The aim is to find the acequia, which starts slightly above and to the right of the scattered oaks. It runs along the NE side of the ridge from about contour 1580m. Cross the track and climb to the nearest oak.

Follow the broken wall which leads on from the tree and after about 100m when just losing sight of the tree behind, diverge to the right on a sheep path towards the oaks higher up.

The general aim is to walk along the ridge or better, by the acequia, slightly below the ridge on the NE side. The large rounded hill covered with pines, Cerro Gordo, to the north west is the direction.

I hope you find the acequia, (see illustration page 92) as interesting as I do. It is for me one of the main reasons for this walk. The sheer amount of work involved in its construction leaves me wondering, "How?" Not to mention its quality and beauty. End on stone angled into the bed, slightly in the direction of flow lets water pass smoothly without eroding the bed on the steeper sections. Large side slabs hold the water on course preventing its natural desire to flow off the ridge. The Acequia de Mecina used to supply Mecina Bombarón and its higher slopes, now barely cultivated, with water carried from the Río Grande de los Bérchules, 9 or 10km away at about contour

2100m. Following the *acequia* higher, after the stone-channelled section, just before it arrives at Cima del Tejar another understandable technique, that of allowing the water to follow natural features and gullies can be seen.

Once the *acequia* has returned to its more ditch like form, the walker has the choice of following it, the ridge or the shade of the trees on the left of the ridge. Any of these choices leads to the point known as Cima del Tejar (5), where a track crosses the ridge, the highest point on the walk.

5. From the *acequia* turn left. Ignore the track heading north and a second branch with two metal gate posts.

6. Take the fire break which is to the left of the tracks and heads down to a wire mesh gate at the junction of two fences within about 50m of the ridge. Looking along a line from the fence to the village of Bérchules, a white painted *cortijo* and concrete water store can be seen. This Cortijo de Montero (7) is the next target.

    Turn right along the lower side of the fence and take the vague track left after about 30m. Follow this track/path for about 0.5km along the lower side of the fence. It then curves downhill away from the fence towards the now clearly visible concrete water store a little below. Join the track below and turn left. After about 1km, the track arrives at the Cortijo de Montero, mentioned earlier.

7. Opposite the small outbuilding is an opening in the fence giving access through to a faint grass-grown track on the lower side.

    Once through the fence and on the path/track follow it down to a wire mesh fence and gate.

    After the gate follow the lower side of the wire to the right. The route has now rejoined its outward path and it will be retraced to the village.

    When the wire fence turns back uphill, the route turns left, downhill following the wall down to the splendid *era*.

    Turning right just above the *era* the path leads on down the stone zigzag path to the river bridge.

    Once across the bridge it is possible to follow the river down a little to find shade, rest and possibly a natural bath if you feel the need. A larger, man made dam feeds a concrete *acequia* and makes a large pool which although not so attractive for bathing does attract wildlife if you wait and watch.

    From the bridge a last slog of 20 minutes or so returns to Bérchules through its *vergeles*. Depending on the season it might be possible to fill pockets and/or mouths with chestnuts, walnuts or mulber-

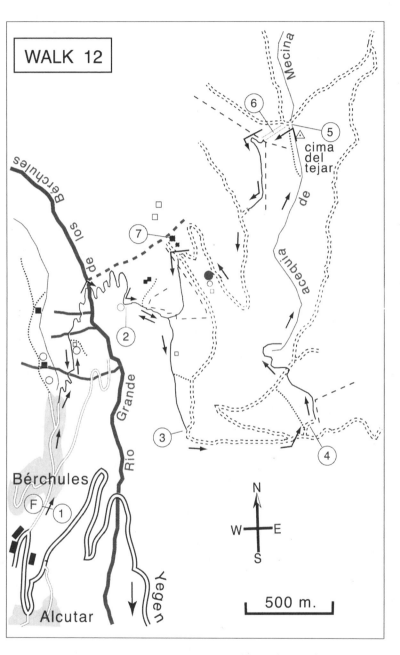

ries on the way. The only snag with mulberry being that on entering the village bar for end of walk refreshment, the evidence of
bright red juice stains will probably be all over hands, face and
dribbled down the shirt into the bargain. Worth it though.

13. A long day in the Río Grande

A long walk, probably of more interest to those who like things to be a little on the wild side. Chance meetings are unlikely, so let someone know where you are going. A really scenic walk, with plenty of shade on the way up to ease the pain.

Time: 7½ to 9 hours plus stops. Start early and make sure there are enough daylight hours. If required, perhaps because of snow on the ground, the highest section can be omitted by walking the track between points (4) and (6), instead of the section of *acequia*. This can shorten the route by a few kilometres.

Waymarks: The route follows Walk 12 in reverse as far as Cima del Tejar. The GR7 waymarks seen are incidental and not always to be followed.

The map for Walk 12 gives more detail of this walk's early stages.

Difficulties: No defined path from point (5) to the track on the descent. The **Notes** mention landmarks that are always clearly in sight except in low cloud conditions. In bad conditions use the track from point (4). Carry plenty of water, none is encountered until late on in the walk.

1. Follow the **Notes** for Walk 12 as far as point (2).

2. From the *era* continue to follow the path uphill and turn right when meeting the wire fence.

   After about 100m the fence makes three right angle bends in quick succession. Follow the vague track that passes through the fence in one of its angles. Ignore the more obvious path heading away from the fence. The track/path leads to a well-made track at Cortijo de Montero.

3. Follow the track uphill, passing a concrete water store on the right. On the following hairpin bend it is possible to see on the sky-line, a prominent sharp crag poking out from the pines. To its left, there is a lower pass through the ridge. This is the target, Cima del Tejar.

   Take a vague track right, uphill steeply towards the tree line. Turn left along the fence and follow the path to where it arrives at the lower end of a fire break passing up onto the ridge. There is a wire mesh gate through the fence at the junction of fences.

   Head up the fire break onto the ridge where there is a confluence of various tracks and the *Acequia* de Mecina, which here looks like a natural eroded gully.

   It is worth climbing a few extra metres onto the rocky peak at Cima del Tejar to take in the scene.

Nearest, on this ridge to the North is Cerro Gordo, a minor peak at 2095m. Clockwise around the horizon can be seen, San Juan (NNW), 2786m, followed by more distant peaks of the Eastern Sierra Nevada, the Sierra de Gador (SE) 2200m, then the sea and the Sierra de la Contraviesa (S) with two outstanding peaks of Cerrajon (SSE) 1508m and Cerro de la Salchicha (SW) 1538m. Finally the Sierra de Lujar (SW) crowned with its communication masts, rises to 1824m and to the west the nearby valley side of Bérchules obscures the highest of the Sierra Nevada.

Cross the *acequia* and follow it through the pines to the left. The route follows this section of *acequia* for about 4km to where it meets the major forestry track. Don't be confused into following any of the branch *acequias* heading off the main one. Keep heading generally north.

Towards the end of this 4km stretch is a double width stone bridge over the *acequia* to the other side. Cross here to put the *acequia* on the right and use any convenient sheep track rising gently up to meet the track.

4. Turn right along the track until finding where the *acequia* crosses it at a point where there is a water store behind a wire fence to the left of the track.

As mentioned in the introduction to this walk, if conditions are bad or there is a shortage of time it is best to turn left along the track to find point (6) instead of continuing along the acequia.

Choose a route following the *acequia* northwards. After a short distance the left bank or indeed the *acequia* itself become the best options. This section is still used, so walking in it may not be an option but it is noticeable that it is much more verdant.

The peak of Cerro Gordo has now been left behind and so the vista to the west has opened up more and at one point the, normally snow covered, peak of Mulhacén (3482m) pushes out over the nearer ridges on a bearing of 280°. The ridge to the east of the *acequia* is that used by Walk 17 described under the chapter "Mecina Bombarón" and the fire break above the *acequia* at this point would join with that route.

The *acequia* continues up into the river bed at about 2100m but this route turns down from it before reaching that point. Cerro Gordo, which from the south looked like a gently rounded fat lump looks very different from the north. Its fierce craggy cliffs falling down into the valley forming a dramatic side show for the remainder of the walk.

Lepidopterists and botanists will enjoy this section of *acequia*. It has a natural look about it. A variety of habitats in sun and shade, damp and dry provide a good selection of flowering herbs to attract butterflies which congregate in clouds to drink at the damp patches left in the *acequia* bed.

Look for an area of flatter land below the *acequia* which has two *cortijos* and two *albercas* nestled in it. The descent begins at a metal sluice gate (5), centrally placed above the two *albercas*. There is also a useful spring in the bank above this point. The left-most cortijo has a track rising up to it and the descent will use that.

5   From the sluice gate there is no well defined path. Take a gradual angle down to the upper side of the left-most *alberca*. Negotiating a broken down wire fence, pass to the left of the *alberca* and to the left of the enclosure surrounding the *cortijo*. Pass around the fence to join the track leaving the *cortijo*.

The track comes to another *cortijo* near which it passes through a usually locked gate. Take the path to the right of the gate. It follows the fence and then zigzags down to the main forestry track.

Turn left up the track. Pass the start of the track that leads up to the locked gate.

6   Take the indistinct path which angles down into the Scrub Oaks, southwards. It is about 50m away from the branch track, about half way along the straight section of track. In 100m it comes down to a barbed wire fence. It follows it.

It crosses a normally dry gully then rejoins the wire fence, descending gently. It crosses two more *barrancos* which normally carry water. Then zigzagging more steeply down, the path aims for a flat-looking meadow below; it arrives at a ruin and passes between it and its *era* (7).

In the rear of the ruin is a sadly neglected winnowing machine, a modernisation of the traditional method of throwing wheat and chaff basketful by basketful into the wind.

From below the wall of the *era* the path heads into the line of poplars, crosses the waterflow and passes down the left of the small meadow to leave it, part way down. The path now zigzags steeply down into the clear area in the river bed. It joins the river slightly downstream from a *cortijo* visible on the opposite side, which has a faint track leading towards it.

Aim for an obvious copse of poplars on the east bank. The path loses itself among a confusion of river meanderings but is obvious again between the poplars and the river.

The poplar copse is about 3 hours slow walk from Bérchules and provides the last good bit of shade for a long stretch. If it is still hot it is probably wise to rest up and eat up, safe in the knowledge that it's generally down from now on; 300m down to Bérchules.

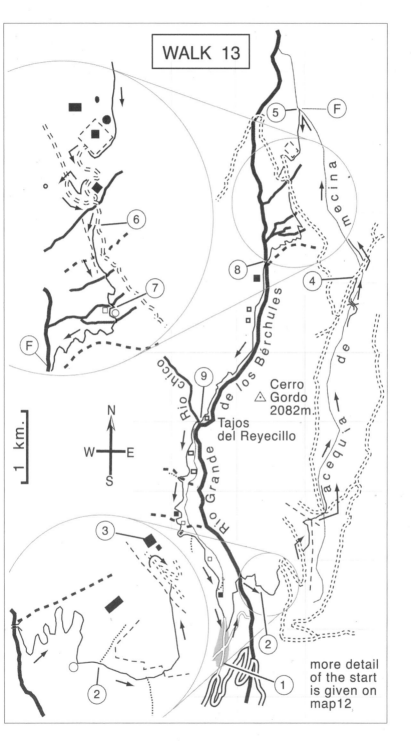

WALK 13

F

5

mecina

6

8

4

7

F

Río chico

9

Río Grande de los Bérchules

Tajos
del Reyecillo

Cerro
△ Gordo
2082m.

acequia de

N
W—+—E
S

1 km.

3

2

2

1

more detail
of the start
is given on
map 12

8. Follow the path which leads out of the poplar copse, crossing the river and leading away down the valley at a level raised above the river bed. It leads under the *Tajo* del *Reyecillo* to arrive at the junction of the Río Chico and Río Grande about 3.5km down the valley.

The cliffs opposite the path provide a stunning backdrop; their angled strata providing enough perches for trees to add to the picture without obscuring. Somewhere amongst this mass of inaccessibility is the cave that provided a refuge from which to wage guerrilla warfare, for Aben Aboo (see Mecina Bombarón). He is the king (let) referred to in the name rey(ecillo).

9. At the junction of the rivers the path crosses over towards the Río Chico tributary and a bridge leads over the river and onto a path following an *acequia* which branches off the Rio Chico.

About 200m along the acequia, in the river bed slightly below is a tempting pool surrounded by worn, smooth rocks. The rocks hopefully hot, ready for flopping on after a quick al fresco bathe.

The path diverges right to a level slightly higher than the *acequia*. The remaining 4km into the village are on this same path which continues obviously on, undulating, but generally down at a level slightly above the *acequia*. There are some turns to the right to be ignored and some minor ones to the left also to be ignored.

On reaching the outskirts of the village at a *fuente* and wash-house take a down-hill road c. Garcia which leads to the various village squares and back to the start point.

14. A Short Stroll above Bérchules

The walk never strays far from the village, passing through the patchwork of nearby plots. Whatever the time of year there will be people working away at something, out and about with mule and mattock. Work may entail quite a lot of sitting under trees smoking but if in possession of a mattock, like the carrier of a clipboard in the corridors of power, one is working.

Time: 2 hours

Notes: There is a whizzy view from the *era* at the high point of the walk and there is scope for delving off on some of the other tracks and paths on the sketch map, to extend the walk if required.

1. Use the village plan on page 79 to find the start of the walk: c. Castillejo. For example: from the bank 20m up from the car park, follow c. Iglesia up to where it joins the main car access road. Turn right at Fuente Platera and keep left until joining c. Nueva. Cross straight over. At the T-junction go right and then hairpin left after 10m. Follow this road to the end of the houses where it degenerates into a path.

    Identify a tall house with the ceramic street name on it 'c. Castillejo No 1'. 20m later there is a *fuente* and a junction of paths.

2. Take the left option at the *fuente*.

3   At the T junction of paths go left and pass an *era* on the left. The path comes to a small *acequia* and bends left at the beautiful bole of a chestnut tree, then 10m later passes a *cortijo* (4).

    100m past the *cortijo*, take the right-hand path which branches steeply up, at another large chestnut tree. The path zigzags up between two wire fences then joins the large ditch of an *acequia*. Turn right along the *acequia*.

    Diverting left along the *acequia* at (5) on a hot day gives a double pleasure of beauty and coolness. An avenue of chestnut trees lines the *acequia* and provides a special place to do what I at least like to do best in these circumstances – sit, watch, think and be cool.

5   After about 80m look out for a path leaving the *acequia*, left, uphill. It is at a point where another path from below, joins the *acequia*. The path zigzags up following a wire mesh fence. Crosses a track and continues following the fence.

6   The fence bends away back downhill but the path continues up in a north west direction. Diverge right to join the track passing the *cortijo* which comes into sight.

7   100m past the *cortijo* at the junction of tracks, go right.

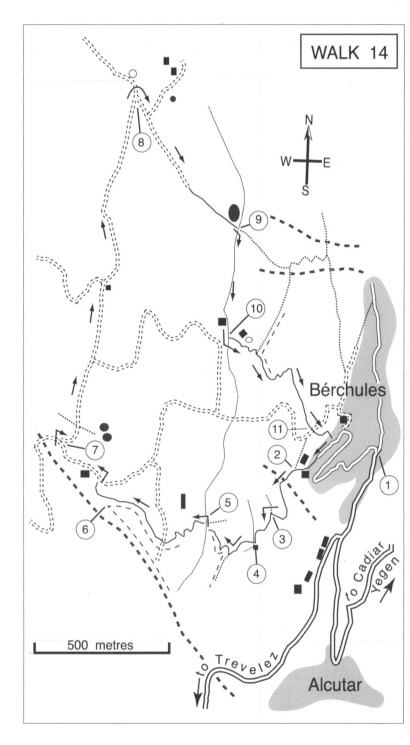

WALK 14

N
W — E
S

Bérchules

500 metres

to Trevelez

to Cadiar Yegen

Alcutar

The track continues on, more or less on the contour, ignore a minor track right. Ignore a left branch at the small building and arrive at the *era* and branch track, hairpin right.

Here is my 'whizzy view', I hope you enjoy it. The evening light sets off the cliffs to good effect. Looking up the Río Grande past the junction of rivers and the Tajo del Reyecillo you can see the area of Walk 13 and higher up that of Mecina Bombarón, Walk 17, leading up to the peak of Peñon del Puerto on the skyline.

8   Take the branch track, downhill, hairpin right, just before the *era* it deteriorates as it descends, passing a ruin on the left and then meets the *acequia* again, just below a large *alberca*.

9   Turn right along the *acequia*. After about 0.5km the *acequia* goes around under a not-very-obvious white-painted house on a higher level. Immediately after the house, a path descends away from the *acequia*.

10 Turn left down the path. Pass the stone *casa de campo* and *era* and continue on the most obvious path ignoring minor branches to meet a track rising from the village.

11 The path continues on the opposite side of the track and leads on to the upper barrio of the village. Following either your nose or the village plan will easily return you to the car park.

A doorway in Bérchules

Mecina Bombarón

Fact File: *Mecina Bombarón*

Buses: Yes, see Appendix A

Taxi: Ask at the corner shop "El Castillo" on the main road between the pharmacy and the town hall.

Accommodation: Yes, see Appendix B

Shops: Supermarket and small food shops. Craft, furniture and nic-nacs. Stamps and postcards in supermarket.

Bank: Yes – no cash point

Medical Emergency: Pharmacy in village. Nearest 24hr centre is Cádiar.

Restaurants: Bar nearest the church is the best for eating. It's normally closed on Friday. Two other bars on the main road and one in Plaza Vieja function for basic *tapas*.

Mecina Bombarón is in itself an unremarkable village, but has been and is the population centre of a fertile valley reaching far up into the Sierra. Famous in the past for its cultivation of apples and potatoes, its valley provided mule routes across to the Granadan villages on the northern side of the Sierra Nevada. Abundant water and some fairly generous areas of flat land encourage a relatively thriving agriculture of cattle, sheep, goats and runner beans. The ancient sweet chestnut trees on the steeper slopes make the valley attractive for walking at any time of the year.

Mecina Bombarón's main historic fame is in being the home of the last Moorish king to claim that title in Spain. In fact Aben Aboo was a very local and short-lived monarch, taking over leadership of the Moorish rebellion of 1568-1571 after murdering his cousin for the honour. He suffered a similar fate at the hands of his own followers, who were promised pardons by the Christian forces of Felipe II in exchange. The fiestas of 'Moros y Christianos' in Alpajurran villages today celebrate, if that is an appropriate word, this bloody rebellion which was, barring future events, the final nail in the coffin of Islamic rule in Spain. (see also Yegen chapter). The drastic ethnic cleansing that followed the rebellion has had a great effect on the development of the Alpajurra that we now see.

15. Both Sides of the Valley

Time: 4½ hours walking, 5 to 7 including rest, picnics, paddling etc.

Notes: Those who prefer walking on well made tracks, to paths of a sheep track nature could use the sketch map to follow the tracks from *El Encinar,* point (5), *to the river.*

Difficulties: The section of the route following the *acequia,* from (13), is often a narrow path with drops to one side. It is not dangerous except to those seriously lacking in agility or who are frightened by such situations. Again the tracks on the sketch map can be used to get back to the village although detracting from the interest of the walk.

1. Leave Mecina Bombarón on the main road, downhill, passing the supermarket, sports surfaces and hermitage.

    On the way down the road, the terrain of the walk is visible ahead. It will pass up the valley on the right-hand side and return on the left. Even at this distance, the difference between the two sides of the valley is obvious in terms of contrasting vegetation, land use and fertility. It is intriguing at any rate to ponder the reasons for such differences between patches of land so close to one another.

    Half a kilometre after leaving the last buildings of the village a track on the right leads down to a group of restored mill buildings visible low down near the riverbed. (usually signed "Puente Romano" and "Los Molinos"). Part way down, keep left at the track junction and continue down to the buildings.

    These nicely renovated mill buildings, (there are two more, further upstream) are available for rent as holiday cottages. Some mill features have been incorporated into the renovation; by peering into the stone arch under the first building one can see the narrow opening from the water reservoir from which water would have shot onto a horizontally mounted paddle wheel. A vertical shaft from this would have been directly connected to the grinding stone mounted on the floor above.A ceramic plaque on the building below quotes the 1491 treaty between the conquering Catholic monarchs and the last Moorish ruler of the Kingdom of Granada. The Alpujarra was to have been the last refuge of the Muslim way of life in Spain in perpetuity.

    The path branches left, off the track, to pass immediately in front of the first building. It continues around the side of the mill and on to the bridge credited with Roman origins although I expect 2000 years of life have seen it washed away more than once.

    Cross the bridge and follow the track up to the main road. At the road notice a chestnut tree on the skyline 50 metres directly above. The path passes this within a few minutes walk.

    Turn right up the road and pass the *fuente* on the left.

2. Look for a stone-laid path on the left just before the first bend in the road. Turn left onto the path.

    The path soon becomes confused among various sheep paths but by concentrating on the chestnut tree noted earlier and by ignoring all the steep uphill options the good path will be rejoined. The path descends a little to a level patch on a rocky promontory with three almond trees, after which it ascends towards the previously noted chestnut tree.

    From now on some yellow/white waymarks may be seen. The path zigzags around the chestnut tree and continues always upwards; usually gradually but sometimes more steeply and zig-zagging.

    At one point, zigzagging up from a promontory from which all three renovated mills can be looked down on, on the other side of the valley, the path comes within sight and hearing of the river for the first time. From this point onwards a dark green patch of woodland comes in and out of view on the skyline, (at about 20°). This is the Holm Oak Wood, *El Encinar* (5), through which the path passes later.

    Five or ten minutes walk after noting the previous point the path is obscured a little by a growth of holly oaks and a small rock fall. The path passes on the uphill side of the holly oaks and immediately becomes more obvious.

    Passing over a shoulder of the hillside after another zigzag section, the Río Mecina can be seen and heard in the most attractive part of its valley. Low down, the line of the *acequia* leading to the mills on the opposite side can be seen passing through the chestnut woods and agricultural clearings. Higher up and depending on the season, are snow covered hills, pine forests, water tumbling down the gullies from melting snow and springs, yellow patches of gorse and broom, dark green of the oaks and amongst all this the music of water and goat bells. Along the line of the path 'El Encinar' can now be seen much more obviously.

3. The path enters a much more open area, the crags on the right have been passed and it descends a few metres into an area of scrub (*adenocarpus*, gorse, bramble, reeds and a few scattered chestnut trees). This is sometimes a bit overgrown but the oak wood is clearly visible as a target ahead.

    Adenocarpus or rascavieja. Adenocarpus is quite a feature of this landscape in April. It is a broom like shrub, which has the characteristic of bearing its brilliant yellow clusters of 'sweet pea' shaped flowers on the tips of its branches giving the appearance of having been decorated with fairy lights, perhaps to celebrate Easter. It is also intriguing for its local name of rascavieja. Depending on the interpretation this could mean 'scratchy old thing' which it does not seem to be or it could be a 'tool' for scratching old ladies. I prefer the latter and during lonely, hallucinatory walks I see the hillside scattered with old ladies in black, smiling ecstatically having just put their yellow, flowery *rascaviejas* to good use.

Emerging form the scrub, aim just to the left of the now visible ruin.

4. Cross two, normally dry gullies, ten metres apart and follow the second gully uphill. The path does go through the reedy patch where there is a spring and pool. If it is too wet or overgrown it is easily circumvented by diverting 25 metres to the left and rejoining the path, visible as a badly eroded zigzag of stone climbing from the spring towards the oak wood.

    Sitting here alongside the spring and its pool for breakfast is often rewarding in that wildlife seems to like the spot as a watering hole, it attracts bird species you wouldn't expect to see on a dry hillside, as well as those you would. A selection of warblers, including dartford, seem to like the reeds; stonechat, ring ousel, woodchat shrike, wheatear are regularly seen. With binoculars you may also be lucky and see ibex, which are often on the cliffs under which the path passes.

5. Pass through the oaks taking advantage of the shade, venerate them for having survived the last century and encourage them to withstand this.

    An eroded track passes through the wood, cross it twice and continue up through the wood. Higher up the trees get smaller and scrubby, those on the left overlooking the valley, dead and dry.

6. The various paths through the trees gradually converge near the escarpment edge between the clear ground and the scrubby oaks.

    Keep the Mecina valley visible on the left and work more or less along the contour at the edge of the trees. The path then becomes clear linking various ruined *cortijos* on its way up the valley.

7. Pass a pair of ruins and an *era*, between the lower ruin and its *era*.

    The next ruin is now visible ahead. Go to it.

    Pass on to the next ruin 30 metres further on.

    50m further on at a higher level is the next ruin to go to.

    The next ruin is now visible by a large chestnut tree.

    Pass on to the last ruin now visible at a lower level 100 metres away.

8. From this last ruin can be seen, about 80 metres vertically below, Cortijo de las Hoyas set in a large flat meadow, with a track rising

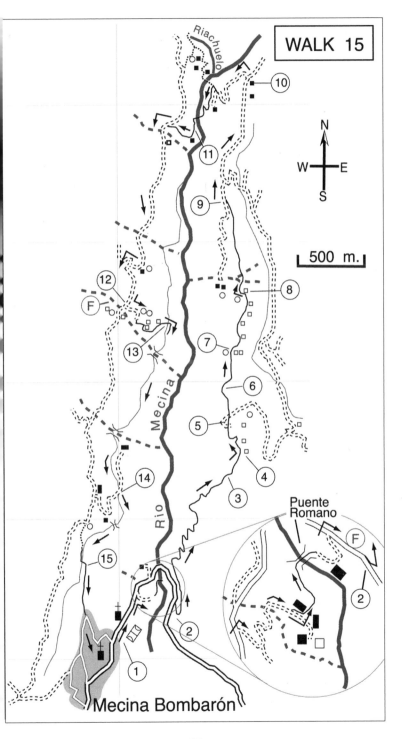

WALK 15

N
W E
S

500 m.

Riachuelo

10

11

9

8

F

12

13

7

6

5

4

3

Mecina

Puente
Romano

F

2

14

Rio

15

1

2

Mecina Bombarón

away from it. Descending 30 or 40 metres towards the crag and *era*, reveals a path heading right, slightly downhill, round into the *barranco*. It crosses one division of the *barranco* through scrub and continues slightly downhill. A second division of the *barranco* usually has water flowing in it and the route climbs a little after this into a scrub of oaks and gorse. The path is vague through this scrub. Take the line of least resistence, following sheep tracks generally on the contour, and the rising track will be met.

9. Turn right up the track and left at the junction of tracks a few minutes walk further on. Descend on the track into the pines where it passes a white-painted *cortijo* with the name plate "Prado Dorado".

   The view from here is up the two branches of the Río Mecina. The right fork being the main river, the left its tributary, Río Riachuelo, they join just below "Prado Dorado". On the opposite side of the valley are visible many *prados dorados*; the pastures are usually golden brown with dry grass rather than green with fresh growth. Exploring the junction of the river and the *Barranco de Riachuelo*, although off the described route, is worthwhile but will probably involve wet feet.

10. From the Prado Dorado outbuilding take the left fork of the track and follow it down until in sight of the stone-built goat corral to which it leads.

    An older, green path/track leads off right from the newer one to the corral. Take the right option, and 20m later the path, hairpin left, that leads down to a footbridge over the river.

    Note: If time and events have taken their toll and the bridge has gone there is another crossable point upstream shown on the sketch map near the junction of the rivers. It is easier to paddle across at this point.

11. Follow the path from the bridge up to and past the upper side of the *cortijo* then turn left along the track joined. Follow the track for about 1 km and at a junction where there are a *cortijo*, *era*, and fenced *alberca*, turn left.

    About ½ km further on look for a minor track on the left (12) with yellow/white waymark painted on a rock. The track leads down to two *eras* side by side. To help locate this track, it is immediately before the point where the main track curls around a wooded *barranco*. On the far side of this there is a stone ruin on the left of the track and, raised on the right, a ruin with a very impressive chestnut tree and *era*. There is also a useful spring in the *barranco* 20m up from the track if you need fresh drinking water.

12. Go left down the branch track to the two *eras*.

    One wonders why two eras. These are beautiful examples and as usual I can't resist their magnetism. I have to stand on the central point, admire the workmanship. Stand, stare and contemplate. Eras are, perhaps literally, magical places; smoothed and polished by centuries of use by threshers and winnowers, they provide welcoming space for dancers, lovers, cavorting witches and daft walkers. But why two in the same place? No obvious reason until you know that these are built either side of a property boundary, each owner wanting and needing his own, in the same windy spot. However inconvenient it might be, the prime consideration for siting an era is the likelihood of catching the wind or breezes passing up or down the valleys. They are often in very inconvenient places, well away from the harvesting, the *cortijo* and mill, but they have to catch the wind. It's ironic that even though the threshing might continue in a time-honoured way, the winnowing process has nearly always been 'modernised' by the use of a hand-operated wind-making and sieving device. I was once delighted to see a 'wind stop work' situation where the real wind blew too strongly into the mouth of the machine for the man turning the handle to compete with. Well, I mean, what could we do, apart from adjourn to the lee of a heap of threshed straw, wriggle the bum onto a nice warm smooth era slab and finish off the wine. But the wine in Spine is never finished!

The track continues past the pair of *eras*, deteriorates to a path and passes to the right of a *cortijo* now used as a goat corral, and on down to pass a stone *casa de campo*. Downhill from the *casa de campo* it arrives at a footbridge over the *acequia*.

13. The route turns to the right and follows the *acequia*. This point is about 1 hour's walk from Mecina Bombarón and the end of the walk. A good place for a last rest, sit in the shade, finish off the picnic and enjoy the scene for as long as you have time for.

Continuing along the *acequia*, pass two aqueducts, nicely constructed to protect the *acequia* from damaging storm water flowing down the *barrancos*. If a lot of water is flowing take care in crossing, the stone work will be slippery underfoot and there is quite a fall from the *acequia* down the bank.

14. The *acequia* meets, passes under a track, and continues on the far side. Keep following the *acequia*. Ignore a footbridge crossing the *acequia*. A path comes down from above to join the *acequia* and both continue on together. 100m later the path drops below the level of the *acequia*.

15. Follow the path not the *acequia*. A few 100 metres later the path enters the village. Any route downhill will arrive at the main road through the village. Staying on the highest street along the top of the village leads to the Plaza Vieja and the chance of refreshment either from the fountain or the bar before dropping down into the modern world.

16. The Acequias

The walk gives an insight into how well the Alpujarreños have taken advantage of available water. Some of the *acequias* will certainly have been in use for 1,000 years, maintained every year to keep them flowing. The mills are of a low-tech Moorish design that had proved itself effective up to the recent past. The walk is fun at any time of year but better in spring and summer when the *acequias* are in use.

Time: 3 hours walking, 4 or 5 hours for those who take their dawdling seriously.

Note: There is a good place in the riverbed for a picnic and a long siesta for those who would like a lunch followed by an evening walk. Otherwise it makes a good morning walk prior to *menu del dia* in the village restaurant.

Difficulties: No serious problems but those seriously lacking in agility might be worried by the narrowness of the path alongside some sections of the *acequias*.

1. Leave the village on the main road, downhill past the supermarket, sports surface and hermitage.

2. ½ km after the last buildings and just before the z bends take the track to the left. Just before the track becomes concreted, a path branches left, steeply up. There is usually a painted sign showing this: '*Camino*'. The concrete track is a private one leading to usually locked gates.

    The path climbs up and around a *barranco*, crossing its waters and passing beneath the house before joining the house's driveway just past the lockable gates.

3. Follow the drive up to the house and turn right just as the house is reached onto a path following an *acequia*.

    The building just passed is a restored mill now available as a rented holiday cottage. There is another (4) a few minutes walk ahead, and a third lower down that is passed on other walks. The lowest mill has a plaque quoting the treaty made between the Moorish ex-king of Granada and the Christian conquerors. The tone is conciliatory, tolerant, and even generous. Sentiments of 1491, which obviously became diluted somewhat over the next 70 years. The plaque on the mill about to be passed quotes a 17th-century historian's account of events in Mecina Bombarón on the first day of the Moorish revolt of 1568.

    "Those of Mecina Bombarón also rose on that Friday night sacking the church, destroying the retablos and the holy images, smashing the alters and finally destroyed or stole all the sacred objects.

Finding the Christians hiding, they captured them all and ransacked their houses.

In this place the rebels raised their standard of shining red silk bordered with threads of gold and in the middle a castle with three silver towers. This they had kept since the Moorish times." D. Luis del Marmol Carvajal.

The *acequia* appears to end at the mill (4) but only because its route is through the mill mechanism from above. The tower-like structure is in fact a sort of aerial well serving as a reservoir. The *acequia* feeds into this at the higher level.

4. After the mill keep heading uphill slightly until meeting again with the *acequia* and follow it to the point where it joins the river.

    Depending on the state of the river it may be possible to cross and find comfortable picnic spots up or down stream. Again depending on the season the pools that sometimes exist upstream might be tempting for a bathe.

    It is from this point, then, that the water that used to drive the three mills was taken. It powered first one then the following two in sequence with the same water.

5. From the river the route climbs steeply up through the chestnut wood. The start of the indistinct path is about 20m from the *acequia* – river junction, 5m downstream from a yellow/white cross waymark painted on a rock and more or less opposite a path going down to cross the river.

    Take the climb slowly and enjoy the trees. Use the easiest possible zigzags of the path and some white paint waymarks may be seen. If in doubt as to the route or having lost the path (it gets covered deeply by fallen leaves) keep going up and leftish. The target is another higher level *acequia*. After two or three minutes of climbing up from the lower *acequia* a stone-built *casa de campo* will be seen as a target.

    Then, a white painted *casa de campo* comes into sight, which will be left to the right.

    Pass above the stone *casa de campo* and another will come into view above and left. Take the line of least resistance towards it and later the target of a concrete *acequia* 30 metres beyond it. Take another breather!

6. On reaching the concrete *acequia* turn right. Follow it around first one *barranco* and then a second, which has a neat stone aqueduct taking storm water over the top of the *acequia*. If, because of much water, this is difficult to cross it is possible to divert slightly uphill.

Continue along the *acequia* as far as a footbridge (7) and turn left up to a stone *casa de campo*.

The walk can be spun out if required by following the acequia for another 1km approximately to where it meets the river, giving more paddling and siesta opportunities.

7. From the stone *casa de campo* follow the ever improving path up to a large, 2-building, goat corral. Pass on either side of this, the path strictly is to the left, but the right is easier.

Follow the track on uphill passing two very nice eras, intriguingly side by side. Even just writing this I have to stop and take an imaginary break to enjoy my 'era sensations'. The track continues uphill to join a major track.

8. Turn left. The route follows the track for about 2km before branching left down a cobbled path towards the village.

Before bulldozers changed the appearance of things this track and the cobbled path comprised a route known as 'Camino de Guadix', Guadix being a town 40km away as the crow flies on the north side of the Sierra Nevada. Much further away in practice than 40km would suggest bearing in mind the height of the pass (2600m), and the means of transport. Routes such as this had much significance for trade and military purposes throughout the ages until the time of motorised traffic. The 'Camino de Guadix' for example had Moorish fortified settlements at its southern end in Golco and at its northern end in Lantéira. All this of great military significance in the 14th and 15th centuries when Granada had Islamic rulers and the remainder of Andalucia had Christian ones. Again in the 16th century, during the Moorish rebellion based in The Alpujarra against the now Christian rulers of the remainder of Spain. It's an important path.

Within 50m of joining the track (8), there is a ruin on the right with an impressive sweet chestnut tree and *era*. There is also a spring in the *barranco* near the ruin, for a top up of fresh drinking water.

100m or so further on, on the left is a stone *casa de campo* with an *alberca* immediately in front of it. This helps to locate *'El Castaño de Cristo'* (9).

Christ's chestnut tree or El Castaño de Cristo is the tree 10 metres downhill from the casa de campo, which is also blessed with a fairly impressive holm oak. The 1936 civil war in Spain was another period of religious persecution. Depending on your point of view, both by, and against, the Catholic Church. To guard against its possible desecration, the churchmen of Mecina Bombarón hid the church's effigy of Christ in this hollow tree so that in the event of anti-church forces taking the area (or as my informant said "in case the reds came"), at least Christ would not suffer.

9. From *El Castaño de Cristo* it is about 1.5km to the point where the

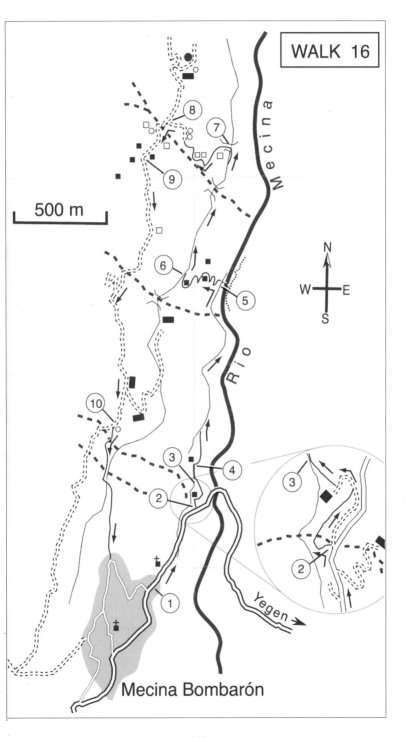

route branches off the main track onto a mule track to the left, and about 45 minutes to the village and the end of the walk. Some landmarks are:

Pass a ruin on the left.

Descend for 50m, cross a *barranco* and climb for 50m. Pass a track to the right at the top of the climb. Keep left.

Pass a new-looking building (goat corral) behind a wire mesh fence on the left.

Pass a track to the left. Keep straight on.

Notice a renovated *cortijo* 50m off the track to the left and then watch out for the first glimpses of the village and a large slightly elevated *era* on the left.

10. Branch left down the path as you pass the *era*, and simply follow the path which has some impressive cobbled sections worthy of El Camino de Guadix and is the widest mule track in The Alpujarra giving room for loaded mules in both directions, a veritable motorway. The path joins the *acequia* again for a while but then crosses it and drops down into the village. Once in the village any route downhill leads to the main road.

A Cántaro (pitcher)

17. Peñon del Puerto, 2750m

Time: 5½ to 8 hours

Notes: The walk is basically a there-and-back one to reach the ridge of the Sierra Nevada by a relatively easy route. It also provides a good access to the more easterly 3,000m peaks of the Sierra Nevada, for those equipped and experienced enough to spend a night or two at high altitude.

Difficulties: Involves 800m of ascent and climbs to an altitude of 2,700m. The walk should only be undertaken from late spring through to autumn before the first snows. Walkers should be experienced in the normal safety and survival procedures used when walking in remote areas at high altitude.

Use the access map (page 106), to reach the start point of the walk which is 20 minutes drive on dirt roads above the village. Drive up hill out of Mecina Bomborón, past the cemetery. 2km after leaving the village there is a broad forestry track, hairpin right. After about 1km, at the first junction of tracks, go left. At 2km, just after the emerging from some conifers, keep to the main track, ignoring minor tracks to right and left and ignoring a left fork. After 4km, ignore a minor track to the right. After 7km, ignore a hairpin left and a minor right fork. Pass a helicopter landing site and a large *alberca* just to the right of the track. The track descends a little through conifers then levels out again. At about 8km, two minor right turns leave at the same point, keep left on the main track. At 9km, there is a firebreak on the left of the track and an *alberca* and *cortijo* on the right. This is the start point of the walk.

> During the last part of the drive up and the first part of the walk while passing through the 'hedgehog zone' of vegetation, an abundance of *Erinacea Anthyllis* can be seen. Nearly all of the leguminous shrubs which dominate this zone are yellow flowered and so it is a special pleasure to see E. Anthyllis scattered liberally over the hillside like blue cushions. Not a cushion you would use more than once, the green parts of the plant are reduced to a dense growth of needle like spines (pointing upwards) as a defence against grazing and dehydration. Beauty and the beast rolled into a happy surprise. The plant had a very localised distribution in south-east Spain, France and north Africa.

1. Follow the avenue through the pines that is found about 50m up the firebreak on the right. The path continues as a visible avenue, crosses two *barrancos* and another firebreak. It continues on the far side of the firebreak to join a higher level forest track.

2. The path crosses this track and continues on the same line but as a well-made track.

3. Within 0.5km the track curves right, but the path continues

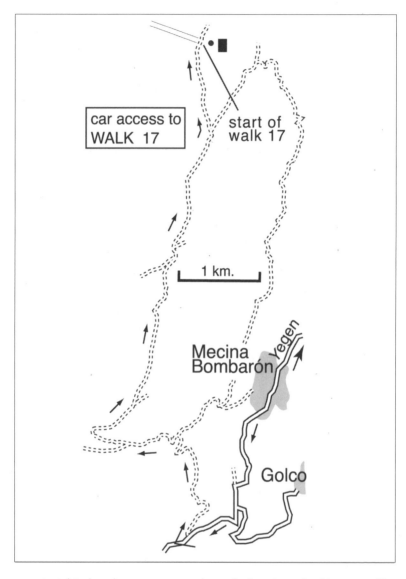

car access to
WALK 17

start of
walk 17

1 km.

Mecina
Bombarón

egen

Golco

straight ahead as an avenue through the pines, looking very like the path taken initially.

The path enters a semi-clearing about 100m across, becomes indistinct but continues on the same line to enter the trees again and become more obvious.

Near the edge of the pines, cross an abandoned *acequia* and head on upwards towards the (blue) sky which signifies the ridge. The

106

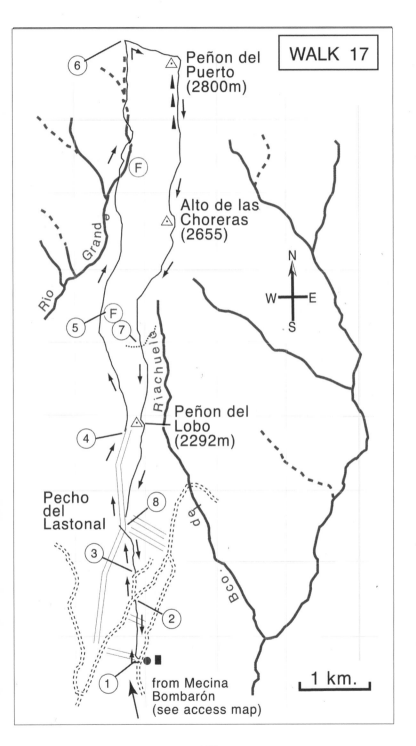

WALK 17

Peñon del Puerto (2800m)

Alto de las Choreras (2655)

Peñon del Lobo (2292m)

Pecho del Lastonal

Río Grande

Riachuelo

Bco. de

from Mecina Bombarón (see access map)

1 km.

ridge is reached more or less at the point where a double firebreak climbing up the hill meets another running along the ridge.

The ridge has been rather disfigured by the firebreak. Opinions differ as to the efficiency of firebreaks. Having seen more than one case where they have failed to break the path of the fire, I lean towards the view that they do more harm than good in encouraging erosion down treeless avenues and being visually offensive. The view from the ridge here is westwards over the valley of Río Grande of los Bérchules, (explored by the chapter "Bérchules") later in its course, Río Cadiar, and later still Río Guadalfeo or "ugly water". Its valley looks fine from here although it's true that from here its waters cannot be seen. This valley and another major one of Río Trevélez separate the viewer from the visible peak (cloud permitting) Mulhacén, the highest of the Iberian Peninsula, and further to the right Alcazaba and a string of other peaks in excess of 3000m.

From this point, (8) Pecho del Lastonal, the route turns right to follow the line of the firebreak. Using either the firebreak or tracks between the firebreak and the trees to the left, made by cattle and sheep, arrive at a point about 50m from the end of the firebreak below Peñon del Lobo (2292m).

4. Take the path which branches left off the firebreak along the edge of the trees.

    Coming to a point where the trees close in on both sides of the path with no obvious was out, keep tending to the right slightly and don't lose height. The path becomes clearly defined later, emerges from the trees and runs along the edge of the thinning conifers.

5. An excellent spring *(fuente fria)* is passed, giving a chance to freshen the water in the drinking bottles. The last of the conifer plantation is reached and the path can be seen running down towards the waters of Río Grande de los Berchules. The rocky nipple on the ridge slightly to the right of the line of the path is Peñon del Puerto but this route chooses to go down to the water-course for fun.

Warning: if the walk is being undertaken in early spring and a lot of snow remains, it is important to note that there is a green area on which to walk at the side of the water flow. If there is not then it is likely that snow is bridging the water flow and the likelihood of falling through snow into water below exists. In these conditions, stay out of the valley bottom.

    Once at water level, cross, re-cross and work up the valley taking the right-hand option of any branches in the ever upward tending valley.

6. The ridge is reached at Collado del Puerto (2621m) and the target of Peñon del Puerto is visible 0.5km to the east. Having taken in the panorama from the peak it is easy (in good visibility) to see the return route along the southwards leading shoulder of hill. In the foreground, three rock pillars in a line about 20m apart point the way towards the rocky outcrop of Alto de los Chorreras (2655m).

A series of fantastic labyrinthine rock 'castles' mark the line of the ridge. Useful to mark the route and fun to explore or shelter in. Ibex seem to like them to hide in and may surprise the walker and/or vice versa.

Continue along the ridge without losing height to the left or right. In bad visibility, it is useful to remember that the upward route taken earlier is never more than 0.5km on the right and that a bearing of a few degrees west of south is correct.

7. At one point where the trees spread over onto the ridge a path heading east-west is crossed but not followed. Following the ridge southwards, it meets the firebreak just below Peñon del Lobo (2292).

Following the firebreak southwards along the ridge is now the reverse of the upward route.

8. A pair of parallel firebreaks climb up from the left to meet that passing along the ridge. Descend by the same route taken for the ascent. The start of which is difficult to see if not remembered from earlier in the day. It angles down left, from the junction of firebreaks, to a large boulder and on the same line down to the abandoned *acequia*.

The *acequia* is about 40m from the boulder and still within sight of the ridge. To the right along the *acequia* is denser forest to be avoided. The path leaves the *acequia*, stepping down over two or three flat slabs of rock and enters a visible avenue through the pines.

The path gets better, enters and crosses the clearing mentioned earlier in this description. Cross the clearing, continue on to join the track. At the track junction, cross straight over to find a continuing avenue which leads on down to cross a firebreak and continue on the opposite side.

On reaching the second firebreak turn left down to the track 50m away – the start and end of today's little adventure.

Yegen

Fact File: Yegen

Buses: Yes, see Appendix A

Accommodation: Yes, see Appendix B

Shops: Yes

Bank: Yes

Cash machine: No

Medical Emergency: Doctor's surgery – Yegen; 24 hour emergency – Cadiar.

Restaurants: All the bars will provide a good value breakfast, or a menu del dia (2pm-5pm). The most comfortable bar is 'Bar Ceci' on the main road. For more varied and up-market dining the 'Bar Rincon de Yegen' has one of the best menus in The Alpujarra and food to match.

Yegen is the most easterly of the Alpujarran villages dealt with in this guide. Apart from the fame brought on it by the writings of Gerald Brenan, it has enough interest and walks around it to justify staying one or two nights.

Brenan was perhaps the first English expatriate to explore the 'year in Provence' genre and wrote, amongst other more serious works on Spain, 'South from Granada', an account of his seven years in The Alpujarra of the 1920's. This book has become the fount of all knowledge for the thousands of immigrants to rural Andalucia, who have followed in his wake. Yegen uses Brenan's fame to the extent of a commemorative plaque on his house and naming a walk after him.

The three walks described are all promoted by the local authority and are, or were waymarked. The waymarks are one of: yellow/white stripes, green/white stripes or red/white stripes with crosses of the two colours indicating "wrong direction". None of the waymarks can be relied upon. The walks here named as they are on the local leaflet.

The third walk, "Las Encinas" can be used to provide a link to walks described in the Mecina Bombarón chapter.

Jeni Robjohns.

18. La Salud (fountain of health)

The walk takes its name from a spring *'Fuente de la Salud'* which sounds marvellous. Unfortunately, there being so many springs in the area I have not yet been able to positively identify 'The source of health'. My suggestion in the mean time is to drink from them all!

Time: A leisurely 2½ hours

Waymarks: Yellow/White – unreliable

Difficulties: No difficulties except the early height gain

1. Leave the village by the main road past Bar Rincon de Yegen, in the direction of Valor (east). Cross *Barranco* de las Eras on the road bridge.

2. 5 metres past the bridge over the next *Barranco* Zajon take the path to the left. The path winds upwards with no surprises passing a *casa de campo* on the right and later another on the left.

   In this section are some impressive evergreen holm oaks (*quercus ilex*) or *encinas* which in the right year and season produce some even more impressive acorns. Try eating a few, they are surprisingly sweet.

3. About 15 minutes after leaving the road, the path joins a track. Turn right along the track then fork left back onto the path after about 20 metres.

   Continuing in a generally north west direction the path comes to a two-storey *cortijo*, bends to the left and continues up the line of a water course amongst sweet chestnut trees.

   It's interesting to see the determined way the ancient chestnut trees cling to their eroded bed. Sweet chestnut trees must, I think, have been the models for those frightening 'big bad wood' scenes in children's stories. These trees would have been much more common in the past. They will have been cleared from the easily ploughed land and neither do they have their old significance as a good building timber and are not being cultivated for that purpose, ferro-concrete being preferred at the moment.

4. About 20 minutes after 3, the path arrives at the dead end of a track. The route turns left along the track. It winds along more or less on the contour crossing three or four small water flows (depending on season), to join at (5) with another track descending from *Cortijo* de Los Alamos, which lives up to its name by being amongst a poplar plantation.

5. Keep left, slightly downhill, southwards. The high point of the walk has been passed and the route now gradually descends to Yegen.

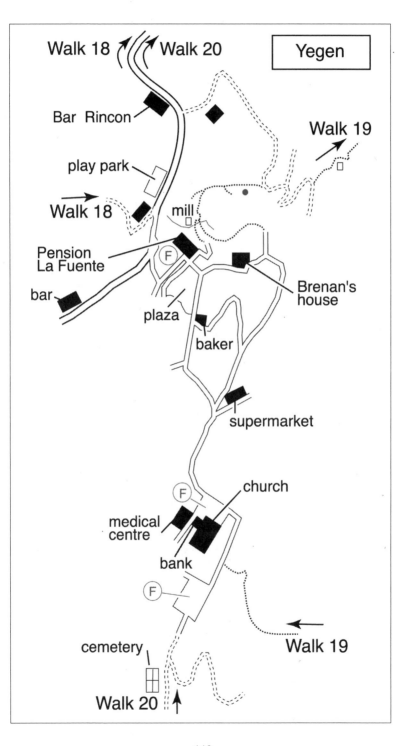

Walk 18 Walk 20

Yegen

Bar Rincon

Walk 19

play park

Walk 18

mill

Pension
La Fuente

F

Brenan's
house

bar

plaza

baker

supermarket

F

church

medical
centre

bank

F

cemetery

Walk 19

Walk 20

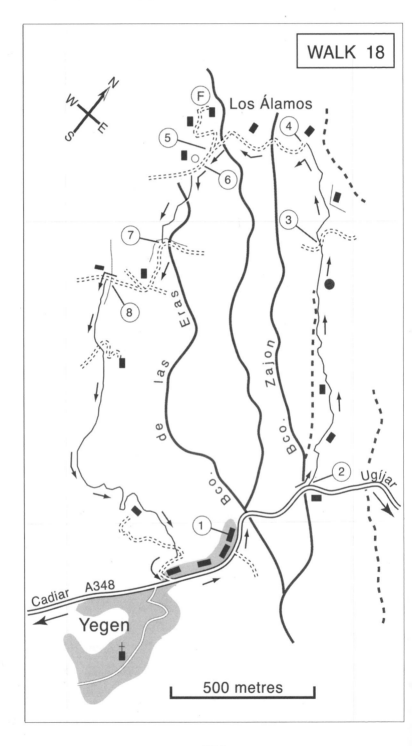

6. Four or five minutes after (5) there is an *era* and a *cortijo* on the right. Branch left onto a mule track here. This path descends, crosses an *acequia* then a stream. Follow the stream for a few minutes before joining another lower level track.

7. Turn right along the track and follow it for about five minutes to a right angle bend at a *cortijo* and minor track branches right and left. After rounding the bend a line of poplars becomes visible ahead, crossing the track. At the same point is a *casa de campo* and a stream flowing under the track.

8. Turn left here down the stone-laid path.

    These stone-laid paths, of which you will tread many in exploring The Alpujarra are a joy to see and tread. They have beauty and function and I can feel underfoot the skill and time given by their constructors in past decades and centuries. Less romantically I can smell the sweat and feel the blisters they must have occasioned. Perhaps not the blisters; having felt a few *campesino* palms, I think they are past blistering.

    This particular path is unusual for being of limestone, much of it tinted pink and purple. It demonstrates very well the danger these paths are in; now often wanted for four-wheeled traffic, it's the work of a few hours with the bulldozer and the driver's whim to destroy a noble piece of work.

    Follow the path from (8) until it joins the main road in Yegen. At one point it cuts across the hairpin bend of a track leading to a *casa de campo*. Ignore the track.

    Later zigzagging a little it passes around the upper side of another *cortijo* and continues down sometimes on a newly bulldozed track, sometimes not, to arrive at the main road.

    Turning left along the road takes the route back to its start point, Bar Rincon de Yegen – but there are others to try!

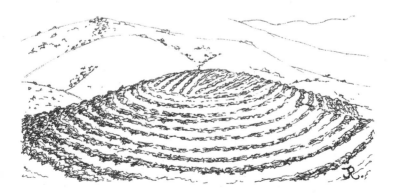

19. Sendero de Gerald Brenan

We are led to believe that this was Brenan's habitual afternoon *paseo* which could well be true. His house is very near to the start of the path and down amongst the lower olive terraces the air would be fresher and cooler than in his house. The described route includes a there and back section to *La Puente* which gives a chance to view at close quarters the 'Land of Grey and Pink' so named by myself for obvious reasons and also one less obvious. It reminds me of a 1970's album cover (Caravan – The land of grey and pink). I wonder if anyone but me bought it.

Time: 1½ to 2½ hours plus 1 hour for the *La Puente* return.

Waymarks: Green/White stripes, unreliable.

Difficulties: Those lacking agility might need a walking stick or a helping hand on one section where a rock fall has broken the path. Also for a waymarked path so close to the village it is surprisingly difficult to follow.

1. From the information boards on the main road go down into the village on the steep concrete road. Ignore a small street on the right and arrive in the *plaza* by Bar La Fuente (2). Refer to the village plan (page 113).

2. To find the start of the path turn left as you come out of the bar, take the second exit from the *plaza*, pass Brenan's house with its ceramic plaque then the first street to the left, under the *tinao*. The street becomes a path curving round to the left.

    Ignore a path to the right. The earth path passes behind and slightly below the backs of the village houses to pass a few metres from a disued mill. Ignore the left branch at the mill, which leads back into the village.

    Turn right to cross the water issuing from the mill and follow the main path to arrive after a few minutes at a rock labelled "Sillon del Moro". A few metres further on the route passes a small *alberca* and joins a track (3).

Be careful now or you will miss the path where it leaves the track at (4).

Take time on the way down the track to spot 'Peñon del Fuerte' which is on the route (6). It is a large flat-topped outcrop in the valley below looking like a jelly moulded by Mrs Giant, it was in its time a Moorish fortification. (More information on the Giant family under walk 24).

From above, three different mounds and levels can be discerned, including an external ring marking the position of its external defence.

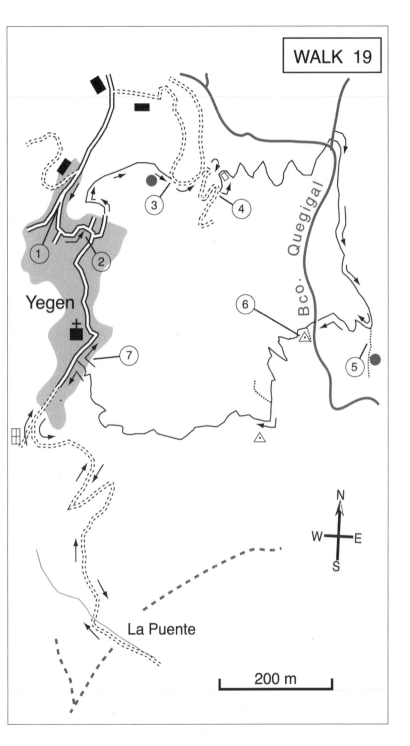

WALK 19

Yegen

BcO. Quegigal

Yegen

La Puente

N
W E
S

200 m

Various civilisations have taken advantage of the site. Prehistoric, Roman and late Middle Ages artefacts have been found apart from the Moorish of the early Middle Ages.

It is rather odd, seeing a fortified hill surrounded by higher ground. Once there however, one realises that any massed attack on that terrain would be fairly difficult and in pre-artillery days it would have been relatively secure. No doubt exists that it did eventually fall.

3. Turn right down the track and after a minute or two it divides. Take the right, downhill, hairpin option. On the next right-hand hairpin look over the edge of the track to spot a small ruin and a path going past it.

4. Take the path left which leaves the track on the bend and drops down to pass the ruin mentioned above. After the ruin the path drops quite steeply into Barranco de Quegigal where it crosses the water and climbs a little to follow it in the downstream direction.

5. At this point the route turns right onto a less obvious path.

If you find yourself passing an alberca, go back about 30 metres and look again.

The path winds through olive and almond terraces and is some-times not obvious. At one point here, a rock fall has made it a little difficult to negotiate. By keeping the *barranco* on the right visible and the position of Peñon del Fuerte (6) in mind, you will not go far wrong.

The path comes back down to stream level and approaches 'Cas-tle Rock' through (in February) a moat of brilliant pink almond blossom which isn't much use for defensive purposes but is very pretty.

6. 'Peñon Del Fuerte'. Arriving at the base of the rock, with its name plaque, a path to the left leads onto the top, for a chance to be king and perhaps feast a little, while to the right is the continua-tion of the walk. The path back up to the village is quite steep but poses no problems, taken slowly. Keep to the most obvious path.

    After ascending to an obvious crag there is a T-junction of paths. Go left towards a flat meadow at the base of the crag. Five more minutes walk from here brings one to the lower *barrío* of Yegen, where there is the option of going directly to the bar or continuing to view the Land of Grey and Pink.

7. Turn left to follow the road out of the village towards the ceme-tery. A few metres before the cemetery take the track forking left which leads after about 1 km to La Puente, mentioned by Brenan as on his route to Ugijar, and the Land of Grey and Pink.

    Return by the same route to (7) and continue uphill through the village to arrive back at the start point.

20. Las Encinas

A circular walk through very beautiful and varied terrain, passing through the villages of Yegen, Mecina Bombarón and Golco.

Mecina Bombarón with its bars and shops makes a good lunch stop. To cut the walk short by stopping at Mecina, time it so as to be able to catch the bus back to Yegen, (11.30 or 20.15), or use the taxi operated by the shop, (see plan page 120).

Time: 3½ to 4½ hours for Yegen – Mecina Bombarón; 1½ to 2½ hours for Mecina Bombarón – Yegen; 5 to 7 hours total circular route.

Waymarks: Waymarks exist but cannot be trusted: yellow/white to Mecina then red/white Mecina-Golco-Yegen. The red/white GR7 markers are much more reliable.

1. Follow the route described for Walk 18 "La Salud" up to (5).

5. Where the tracks join at the acute angle take the hairpin, right, option.

   Following the track, pass the cortijo on the left.

   Pass the track branching right to Cortijo de Los Alamos and a few metres later take the right-hand track branch to arrive at (6), a point where the track has now deteriorated to a sheep trail and crosses a water flow from various springs.

6. Cross the water before angling to the right, climbing, with the poplars being left to the right and below.

7. The now very poorly defined track meets a gully (sometimes carrying water), crosses and turns left, upwards, to follow the right side of the gully. After a few minutes it passes around the head of the gully.

8. The route now climbs less steeply across the face of the hill on a bearing of about 245°. There is sometimes a 12v. electric fence to cross here, no problem if covered with a coat or similar.

9. At the fence look out for a few poplar trees on the skyline, they are the target. The route also follows the line of some metal covers marking the line of a buried pipeline.

   Fifteen minutes walk from the wire fence, will bring you to the track near a junction. Take the left fork or follow the water course cutting across the loops to arrive at a point about 50 metres below *El Molino* La Señal (10).

   El Molino La Señal is the highest point on this route at about 1600m, more than 1000 feet of climbing since leaving Yegen. It provides a pretty good panorama and some grassy spots for resting and snacking.

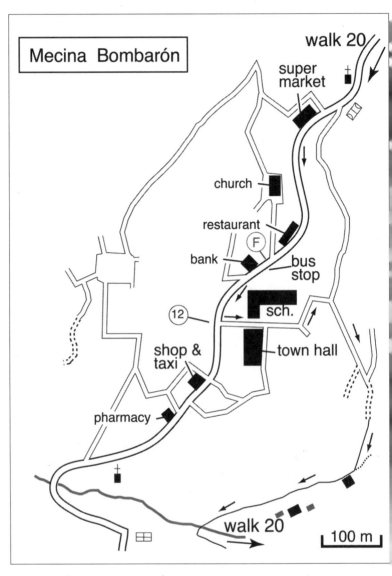

Mecina Bombarón

walk 20

super market

church

restaurant

F

bank

bus stop

12

sch.

shop & taxi

town hall

pharmacy

walk 20

100 m

Although there are now modern concrete *acequias* leading water to the mill and on down towards the village, the original mill *acequia*, nicely constructed and comfortably grassed over, can be found to the left of the building, between it and the track. It would have brought water to the mill from a point where the Río Mecina, running in the valley to the West, crosses the 1650m contour. The *acequia* at the mill seems to be running the wrong way this may be an illusion or it might be the reason for its concrete replacement.

There is much discussion over the concreting and tubing of *acequias*.

These days of cost consciousness make pipes and concrete cheaper than maintaining hand-hewn channels. From an ecological point of view, what is overlooked by the accountants is the good effect of filtration from an earth channel into the hillside along its total length. Pipes and concrete add to the desertification effects of climate, grazing and poor management.

On the walk up from Yegen patches of green hillside can sometimes be seen with very dry dead patches above or below them. There is often a black plastic pipe across the dry section depriving it of its natural supply.

Looking south-east from the mill gives a bird's-eye view of weird erosion effects. Later, the walk passes through some of this 'Land of Grey and Pink' between Golco and Yegen. According to some sources (i.e. Brenan since we're on his patch) the depression below us, in some distant geological period formed a lake bordered by the coastal range visible to the south and these lower slopes of the Sierra Nevada from which we see it. The deepest part of this lake we see below Yegen and around Ugíjar and the fine silt which mounted up in its bed, hundreds of feet thick, now forms the red and grey cliffs and pinnacles also hundreds of feet high in some cases. The cliffs and shaping are largely the effect of a sudden draining of the lake to the sea, which scoured the soft but cohesive sediments to more or less their current fantastic forms. Finishing touches no doubt added by surface weathering since.

10. At this point a poorly defined track with a chain across, and the path, leave to the left at more or less the same point.

11. The path joins the track after about 50 metres. Follow the track into the next valley where it passes above an *era* and some ruins to enter the holm oak wood that gives the name '*Las Encinas*' to this walk.

The oaks certainly deserve a mention. The dense and dark evergreen forest with a sub-canopy layer of shrubs and small trees is the climax vegetation at this altitude in the Mediterranean region. This particular wood is in a degenerating state, thinning, ageing and on its way to becoming the Maquis and Garique that surround it. In their present mature state the individual trees are magnificent specimens giving pleasure and welcome shade. I usually give them a respectful hug to encourage and thank them as I pass.

Leave the track and wander downhill through the oaks, re-crossing the track lower down and later emerging from the lower end of the wood.

Keeping to the left of a reedy area walk to the edge of the terrace and the path can be seen zigzagging down towards a ruin and *era*. Looking further, the line of the path can be seen slanting down across the face of the craggy hillside on the left of the valley. Further in the distance on the right of the valley can be seen the vil-

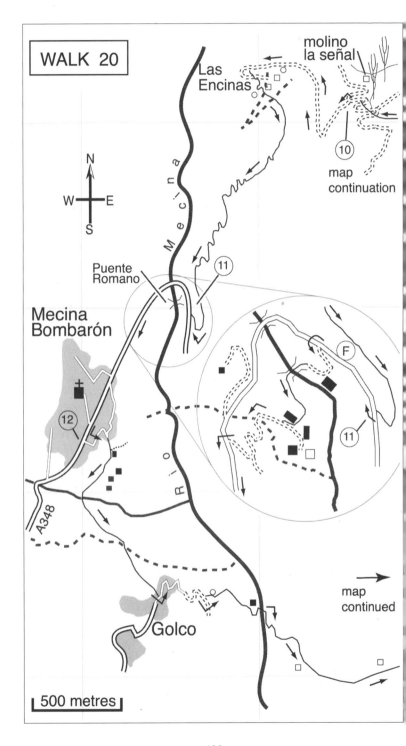

WALK 20

molino
la señal

Las
Encinas

10
map
continuation

N
W — E
S

M
e
c
i
n
a

Puente
Romano

11

Mecina
Bombarón

†

12

A348

R
í
o

F

11

map
continued

Golco

500 metres

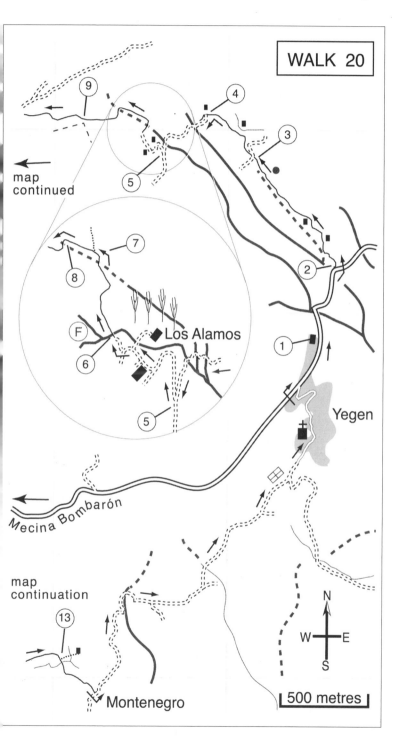

WALK 20

map continued

map continuation

Los Alamos

Yegen

Mecina Bombarón

Montenegro

500 metres

123

lages of Mecina Bombarón and Golco through which the rout passes.

Zigzag down aiming for the right-hand side of the ruin. If the reed patch has become too overgrown or wet it is easy to circumvent to the right. Arrive at the *era* just below the ruin.

Cross two dry gullies just below the ruin, passing above two o three chestnut trees and below another, aim for a patch o broom-like shrubs (*rascavieja – adenocarpus*). After passin through this rather overgrown section the path climbs for abou twenty metres before continuing its long descent into the valley At times zigzagging, and always down, it leads to the main road about forty-five minutes walk from the oaks.

11. Turn right down the road, pass the fuente and notice below th road the Roman bridge over which the track, left, now leads.

After the Roman bridge the path leads to a group of three nicel renovated grain mills available as holiday cottages.

At the mills turn right up the track, ignore one branch to the left and join the main road again. Turn left to arrive in the village o Mecina Bombarón. (See sketch plan page 120)

One of the renovated mills has a ceramic plaque quoting the treaty between the Christian kings of Spain and the newly defeated Emir Boabdil of the Moorish kingdom of Granada.

"Their Highnesses and their successors will always allow the Emir, his governors, bailiffs, chiefs, gentry and commoners great and small to live in his kingdom under his law. They (their Highnesses) will not allow the destruction of mosques and fortresses and will not benefit from taxes due from them, nor will they disrupt the ways and customs of their lives." Ferdinand and Isabella 28.11.1491. Good intentions and amazing tolerance promised providing Boabdil set up house in the outback of The Alpujarra.

12. Leave Mecina Bombarón by the concrete road (calle Iglesia Vieja to the left of the town hall *plaza*. Pass below the school then down hill to take the right fork where it divides. Bear right onto a pat leaving the concrete road at the hairpin bend. (See village plan Between Mecina – Golco – Yegen, at least, some red/white GR waymarks will be seen.

The path soon passes a *casa de campo* and two rectangula *albercas* on the left. Cross a *barranco* with running water and the another dry *barranco* with a rock spine above the path. At th second *barranco* the path divides and rejoins itself and continue on ignoring various smaller branches.

At one point the path divides around a wire-fenced olive grove Take the left path to arrive at Golco where there should be a sig pointing down, left, on a concrete road "Montenegro, GR7 – 50 minutes".

Golco hasn't yet decided whether it is going to continue or die. The church has a lovely tower but looks in imminent danger. The empty derelict school alongside has a plaque commemorating its construction as part of a government school building plan in 1961. It had a short life, no children have been to school in Golco for years. Golco is suffering the fate of hundreds of others, the depopulation, and eventual abandonment due to lack of employment

Turn left down the concrete road leaving Golco. After various hairpins it comes to a picnic area with a spring where it becomes a track.

After a few hairpins of the track the path turns left, off the track, down to an *era*. It crosses the uphill side of the *era* and continues down, past a *casa de campo*, aiming for a copse of poplars in the riverbed.

Cross on the bridge into the poplars, turn downstream and find the path at the lower end of the poplars, sloping uphill onto the low grey cliffs.

After climbing onto the first cliff after the poplars it is possible to see, with binoculars on a bearing of 205°, the remains of Golco's 8th-century Moorish fortress. It sits on a promontory overlooking the route up the riverbed but all that is visible is a section of masonry two or three metres high on top of a shrub grown mound. For the rest we have to imagine.

The path leads on to Montenegro which is no more than a few *cortijos* scattered amongst their olive groves. It is quite and oasis and was property of Aben Aboo. (See Chapter: Mecina Bombarón)

13. Soon after entering the olives of Montenegro there is a branch path off the route to the left. This branch leads to a *cortijo* but before reaching it, it passes a marvellous spring. Lovely place, great water – try it.

Continuing the route, it zigzags a little and soon joins a track. Turn left up the track and follow it, ignoring three minor tracks to the right.

The track passes through the "Land of Grey and Pink", then passes Yegen cemetery. Immediately after the cemetery it is joined by the track from the right leading from La Puente. (Walk 19)

Ignoring the branch to La Puente, a few minutes walk brings you into the lower barrío of Yegen.

Miscellaneous Walks

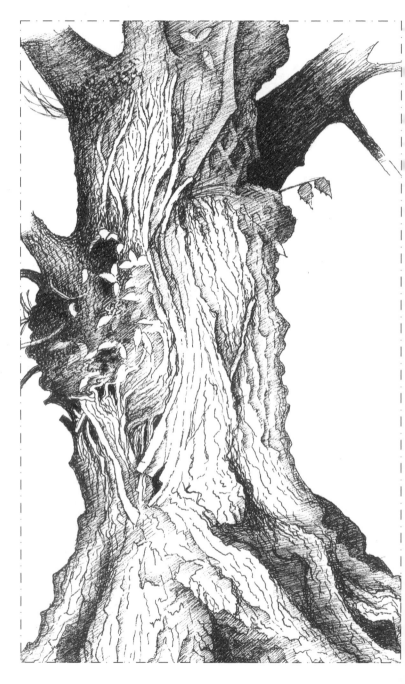

21. Puerto Juviléy

This is a walk for different people in different seasons. Ideal in summer for playing in the river with the children, as a quiet spot for ornithologists and in providing a great variety of bird life attracted to the river for nesting or feeding, and ideal in very early spring for the wild flowers which don't appear until later in the season elsewhere. The walk as described involves walking for about 2km down the river bed, crossing and re-crossing the water repeatedly. Have some rubber sandals if you don't like getting water in your boots, boots are required for the remainder of the walk.

Time: 3 hours walking plus paddling and picnic time

Buses: Buses are used to stopping at Puerto Juviléy. A bus passes from Órgiva on its route to Yegen, see Appendix A.

Notes: No drinking water on route

Difficulties: The circular walk is not possible if there is too much water in the river. If the water is flowing crystal clear and about ankle deep at Puerto Juviléy then there is no problem lower down. A stick makes crossing the river much more secure. It is impossible to predict the extent to which the riverside vegetation has encroached, it depends on the extent of winter storms, if any.

1. Start at the track which leaves the A348 Órgiva – Torvizcón road between km27 and km28. The track branches left and winds down to the hamlet of Puerto Juviléy.

   The track levels off in the valley known as the Rambla de Alcázar where sometimes a lovely stream flows. In early spring the flat, wild, broom-covered areas either side of the watercourse, and the path which short cuts the loops of the descending track, are rich in wild flowers. Orchids of the ophrys genus are common, and truly cute mini, stalkless irises make blue patches among the new grass spangled with the gold dust of dwarf marigolds. In these conditions it is worthwhile wandering around for a while upstream in the rambla to the right of the track.

   Puerto Juviléy has about 15 residents; tucked away quietly here out of sight of the main road, they are able to pretend the rest of the world does not exist. TV and radio signals barely arrive here; electricity and telephone wires don't either, a perfect spot for those content to live in the past.

   Before the 1930s when the only transport up the valley was by mule, the village was on the main route and boasted shops, bars and an inn. The chapel and school room complete with teacher's house was built in the 1940s when there were about 20 pupils. Two or three families still practise their self-sufficient life style as can be seen from the well-cared-for plots alongside the river.

The *posada* where travellers would have rested with their stock overnight is the building with the large arched doorway to a covered courtyard at the top of the cobbled roadway.

2. Once in the riverbed, turn left, downstream. There is no defined path, the route follows the watercourse for about 2km crossing the flow where necessary.

Until you know how strong the water is, be very cautious. The water flows fast and although it may not be deep it can have surprising force. Face upstream, use a stick for extra stability, take small steps and don't hurry. If in doubt give up and go back.

The river makes a right-angle bend under a cliff with a modern house on top of it. 30m later there is a ruined mill on the right.

100m later there is normally a broad gravelly area on the right bank and a few metres downstream another on the left.

Immediately after these the usual course of the river is behind a bamboo and oleander screen. There is in some years a natural pool here, a good place to dilly-dally.

Terrapins inhabit this stretch of the river and from about Easter onwards they are very likely to be seen (if they don't hear you first). In early spring they tend to get all silly and are looking for sex and forget their caution, in this period large specimens of up to 15cm can be seen. Later in the summer only the immatures seem to come out, the new year's hatchlings are about 3cm in length.

3. At a right-angle bend to the left and right under high cliffs there is an almond plantation on a flat silt bed, left of the river. The remains of another mill are hidden under a large fig tree here.

About 1km after (3) at the next sharp bends in the river are more cliffs and the point where the route leaves the riverbed (4).

Below (4), about 1.5km down river, is the confluence of the Río Guadalfeo and the other Alpujarran rivers. Between (4) and the confluence the valley changes character, opening out into a wide gravel bed where the river makes numerous channels depending on the amount of water. Time permitting it is interesting to continue down to the confluence which is a beautiful spot.

4. Look for a path or route into the almond plantation to the left. A path rises to a ruin about 100m back from the river. The path continues up from the upper side of the ruin, angling south-east up the hill. It continues without problem back to the main road.

5. Turn left along the main road. The start point is about 1km away.

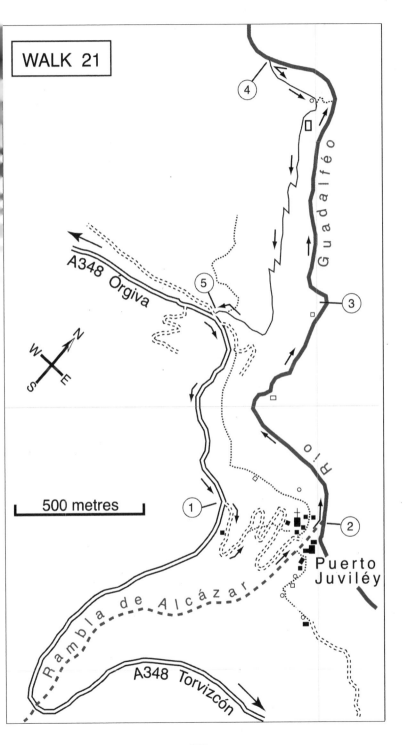

WALK 21

④

⑤

A348 Órgiva

③

Guadalféo

N
W E
S

500 metres

Río

①

②

Puerto
Juviléy

Rambla de Alcázar

A348 Torvizcón

22. Río Guadalfeo, Cástaras and Notaez

The main interests of the walk are to visit the villages and to see the Mediterranean face of The Alpujarra as the route passes almond, fig and olive groves and the different *rambla* terrain.

Time: 4 to 5 hours plus a possible 2-hour diversion

Cástaras: Pensión and a bar but no public transport. The bar marked on the village plan is worth a visit.

Notaez: Shop. No public transport.

Waymarks: Between Cástaras and Notaez the route follows the GR142 and the path is marked with signs and red/white paint marks. Waymarks are not referred to in the text.

Notes: If on arriving at the start it is found to be impossible because of the amount of water it is still very worthwhile taking a look at Notaez by walking up the road and continuing the route from (8).

Difficulties: If there is too much water in the river and it cannot be paddled through safely the walk is not possible. This is obvious from the start point. In normal seasons the river bed is walkable from late spring through to the onset of winter rains. Have water with you at the start, refills available in the villages. Carry food for the whole walk, neither the bar at Cástaras nor the shop at Notaez can be relied upon to be open.

1. To arrive at the start point drive along the A348 Torvizcón – Cadiar road and take the side road between km39 and km40, signed to Notaez. Park near the river bridge. An alternative access to the river is at Cortijo Los Mudicos marked on the sketch map.

   Follow the river upstream (eastwards), crossing and re-crossing where necessary. Just after a large side valley (*Rambla* de Cástaras) look for a track descending from the main road at Los Mudicos. Follow the track up north as it climbs away from the river.

2. The track passes just above a large two-storey *cortijo* and continues climbing. It passes another *cortijo* set in its fig plantation and later a ruin.

   Looking from the ruin a large building with a pitched roof can be seen on the far side of the Rambla de Cástaras. This once thriving and obviously prosperous establishment is known as the Baños de Piojo and is the subject of a diversion off this walk. It is not an easy path and requires a stick with an effective point and a lot of care. The baños went out of use a generation or two ago and the path has deteriorated badly. The spring still flows so it is still possible to take the cure.

   The real reason for going is to visit the well-preserved mule and

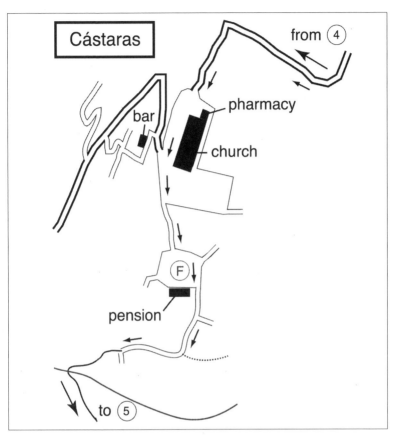

man-powered olive mill and press, which, if you have an interest in such things, will repay the risks of the path. Take care and don't be too proud to turn back if it looks too nasty for you.

The mill functions by the rolling action of conical mill stones on a circular bed stone. The crushed fruit and stones flowed into the circular canal around the bed stone and was then layered between the mats under the press in the adjacent room. See illustration page 75.

The mats themselves are amazing for the amount of work in each one. Many cigarettes, glasses of wine and winter fireside yarns have passed over the plaiting of each of these as well as many hot hours on the hillside picking the grasses.

The track winds but heads generally north. It passes a newly built *casa de campo* on the left and about 0.5km later a minor track branches right. Continue on the major track to the north.

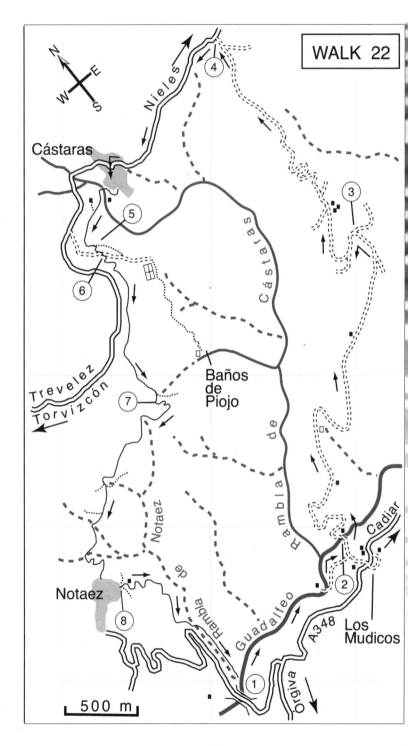

WALK 22

Nieles

Cástaras

Cástaras

Trevelez
Torvizcón

Baños
de
Piojo

Rambla de

Notaez

Rambla de

Notaez

Cadiar

Los
Mudicos

Guadalfeo

A-348

Orgiva

500 m

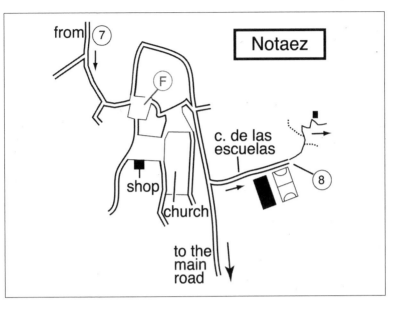

3. At the T-junction of tracks turn left. A few hundred metres later ignore a branch track left, keep right.

    At a group of buildings ignore a minor track left and a few minutes later ignore a minor branch right. Follow the main track as it zig-zags up a steeper section. Follow the track to where it joins the main tarmac road.

4. Turn left and follow the road into Cástaras. Between Cástaras and Notaez the path will follow the waymarked GR142.

    The ruins at (4) are of mercury mine, the recumbent chimney using the same technique as the lead mines of Yorkshire; extra length for extra draught without the problems of building high.

    The church at Cástaras is worth a look in if you can gain entrance. There is a key holder in the village. Like most of the Christian churches here, it was built in the early 16th century, soon after Christian rulers took control of Granada. The main external door is original as is the beautifully worked beamed and latticed wooden ceiling in the mudejar style. This name has come to be given to the architecture of Muslim workers living under Christian control. An interesting interplay of religious tolerance, or exploitation, which did not last. This may be demonstrated by the visibly unfinished ceiling; near the main door is one large panel, which has a degree of intricacy far above the rest. The theory being that the whole ceiling was destined to be completed in this way but politics and rebellion lead to the final expulsion of Muslims, so no one with the skills remained to finish the work after 1571.

All the internal trappings apart from the ceiling date from the 1940s, the effigies and their regal vestments replacing those destroyed by anti-church factions during the civil war. Another phase of pointless destruction by the villagers themselves.

Pass through he two *plazas* of Cástaras and, leaving Pension Maria on the right, turn right out of the second *plaza*. (See sketch plan).

Follow this street to the end of the village where it bends right and leads to a house 100m out of the village. Take the path right just before the house gates. The path leads into a tree-filed *barranco* and exits into an open limestone area. Ignore a path to the right 100m from the *barranco*.

5.   200 or 300m later as the path curves around to the south, take a path which zigzags up right.

6.   The path meets and crosses the concrete road which leads to the cemetery.

If attempting the diversion to *Baños de Piojo* follow the concrete road to the cemetery and then the path which leads away south from the cemetery.

After crossing the concrete road the path continues to rise for a while then levels out and continues as a well-trodden path.

7.   At this point the path crosses a shoulder of hill which tends to get ploughed up and so the path may not be very clear. There is also a minor path to the left to ignore. The path crosses the shoulder between almond trees and the first sight of Notaez is obtained before zigzagging down to the south for a few hundred metres.

After the zigzags, it curls around into a *barranco* gently downhill. At the apex of the path in a *barranco* , ignore a minor path left. Follow the most obviously used path.

At a subsequent *barranco*, ignore minor paths to the left and right. Follow the main path. Later where the path forks, keep left on the more downhill option.

On the approach to Notaez notice the large institutional looking building slightly to the left of the village. This is the disused school and the exit path leaves the village past it. On entering the village keep left to arrive at the village centre.

Spend as long as you can in Noteaz. It is beautifully kept without being untastefully over the top. It is the village that remains most unchanged in a physical sense and also in terms of way of life. The population is dangerously low as shown by the disused school, but it is far from abandoned and depressing as some villages are.

A few years ago a visiting stranger strolling the streets and plazas of Notaez would have been given the suspicious stares due to an alien, but now the villagers are more used to Martians with Leki poles. Try to compliment them on their village and you will be rewarded with a very friendly welcome. The shop is the door to the right of the yellow letter box in Plaza de España.

8. Using the sketch plan of the village leave by c. de las Escuelas. 50m after the school take the left fork downhill. Immediately after that, ignore a left fork and continue steeply down the zigzags to pass a concrete block *casa de campo* 10 metres later.

The path is now easily followed down to where it joins a *barranco* at the base of a cliff of *launa*.

Follow the *barranco* down. It joins the Rambla de Notaez and this or the road can be followed back to the start point.

In the last section of the walk in the *rambla*, all the classic vegetation of these usually dry river beds can be seen. Where the sides of the *barranco* are steep nothing grows on the dry unstable *launa* except perhaps the pioneering caper (*capparis spp*). In other parts the climax vegetation is reached; the broom-like shrub (*retama monosperma*), leafless to preserve water, yellow flowered in spring and with single-seeded pods that rattle in the winter winds.

Rosemary (*rosmarinus officibalis*) and oleander (*nerium oleander*) make a spectacular show in their season. The prickly pear cactus (*opuntia ficus-indica*) has beautiful large yellow flowers and refreshing fruit in summer if you know the techniques of avoiding their vicious spines. The agave (*agave americana*) is notable for its spectacularly quick growing flowering shoot, up to 8 metres in two or three weeks. The tall poles then remain with their dry antler-like side branches until future storms knock them down, the plant dies after flowering, exhausted.

The amount of vegetation in the *ramblas* varies greatly; in a wet stormy winter everything can get uprooted and washed away or buried under new deposits of silt and rock, four or five dry winters can enable a *rambla* to become densely vegetated.

Walk 23. Haza de Lino, Sierra de la Contraviesa

A walk to demonstrate most of the features of the Sierra de la Contraviesa. The cork oaks *(quercus suber)* are more famously found in coastal regions of southern Portugal and south-west Spain; here they are almost coastal, they can see the sea, but are growing at an unusually high altitude. Haza de Lino is the name given to the collection of buildings around the road junction at the start of the walk. The bar, it seems, is an obligatory stop for everyone passing by, it is often an unexpected hive of activity. Its altitude makes it suitable for ham drying which explains the factory-like buildings at Haza de Lino and Venta El Chaparro.

The best specimens of the oaks are near the start and end of the walk, so if need be a shorter version of the walk can easily be devised by using the sketch map. The trees like to grow into "Japanese print" shapes and the trunks have the most fantastic colour orange when just stripped of their cork bark. The colour changes with time and weathering to a red-oxide and almost purple as the bark layers begin to regenerate. In 1995 a disaster in the form of a forest fire struck the whole forest. Amazingly, life remained in most of the trees due to the insulating effect of the cork bark. Thankfully, only small trees and branches were lost.

Other sections of the walk pass through almond, fig and vine plantations and one of the main reasons for doing the walk is to get the best views of the Sierra Nevada. February would be the ideal time for the walk giving foreground views of almond blossom covered hills with the distance occupied by snow-topped mountains against a clear blue sky. Very often as the day progresses cloud forms on the *sierra* down to the snow line, spoiling the view, so it is best to do the walk in the morning.

Time: 4 to 5 hours plus rests

Start point: From Órgiva take the A348 towards Torvizcón and branch right following signs to Albuñol. From Cadiar, take the A348 direction towards Órgiva then A345, Albondon, and turn right at Venta de Tarugo GR443. (See area plan page iv)

Notes: Easy underfoot but rather steep between points (5) and (6)

Difficulties: No water encountered on route. There is a spring slightly off the route, marked on the sketch map between points (7) and 8. The river is usually dry.

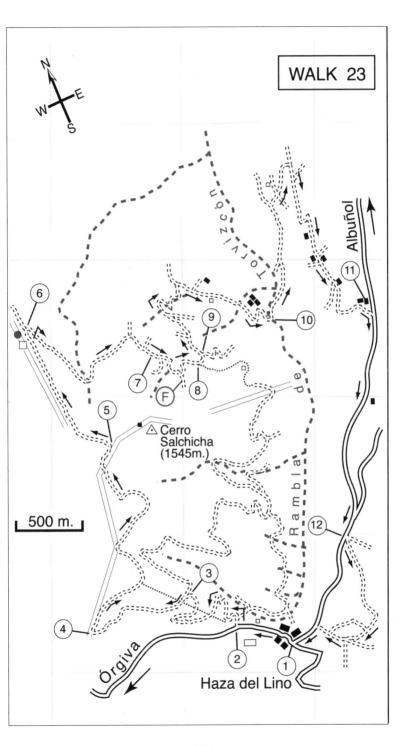

WALK 23

N
W — E
S

Torvizcón

Albuñol

⑥

⑨

⑩

⑪

⑦

Ⓕ

⑧

⑤

△ Cerro
Salchicha
(1545m.)

Rambla   de

500 m.

⑫

③

④

Órgiva

②

①

Haza del Lino

1. From the bar walk west along the road, direction Órgiva.

   Pass a track on the left leading to a large ruin.

2. At the forest track, about 0.5km from the bar turn right. There is a confusion of tracks but the route follows the most obviously well-maintained and used track which has the advantage of climbing more slowly.

3. At this T-junction turn left, still following the main route.

4. The track emerges from the trees and makes a hairpin bend along the edge of the fire break.

   Hopefully it's a perfectly clear day and from around here the proximity of sea and sierra can be easily seen. To the south west the view below is of the rambla heading out to sea at Castel de Ferro, although the town cannot be seen its industry can. The rambla is filled with plastic greenhouses, it looks bad from here and the nearer you get the worse it becomes. The rubbish generated by this agriculture together with the aptitude of the people and their local authorities for turning a blind eye to the problem create what amounts to an offensive fly tip for 100km along the coastal strip to Almería. Expansion of the industry without control has created a hideous plastic desert, which is advancing far faster than any sand one.

   Conditions under plastic are as good for growing disease as for the plants themselves. The plants therefore grow hydroponically in a chemically controlled environment to produce perfect-looking, out of season vegetables by the ship load to supply the supermarkets of Northern Europe.

   To stop the advance of the desert all we have to do is to stop buying suspiciously cheap and good-looking out of season vegetables. Who wants a perfect tomato anyway? Even the bugs won't eat them! Perhaps the sixth sense of the bugs tells them that there exists a "mad tomato disease", I hope there's no truth in my jest.

   The view to the north is more uplifting, as the walk continues you can appreciate the best view of the snowy mountains. In spring it looks perfect against a blue sky.

   Continue following the main track from point (4) as it leads up to a fire watch hut on the peak of the hill (La Salchicha) at 1545m.

5. 100m before the observation hut take a track branching left off the fire break. It's a clear track but the start of it sometimes disappears due to the bulldozing of the fire break. It descends rather too steeply, following the line of a firebreak, towards two concrete water stores visible below.

   Take a break on the way down to take in what can be seen. The valley on the left is the Rambla de Alcazer and a glimpse of the village of

Alcazer is obtained as you descend. It's a valley worth exploring if you pass that way. On the right is the Rambla de Torvizcón across which this route will pass later. Many of the villages of The Alpujarra are spread out on the far side of the wide valley of the Río Guadalfeo. At the extreme left Lanjarón and down low amongst its dark green olive trees, Órgiva. Moving to the right Cañar, Soportujar, Pitres, Pórtugos, Notaez, Cástaras, Nieles and Timar. The villages of the Poquiera valley and Trevélez are hidden in their valleys.

Looking east along the rolling ridges of the Sierra de la Contraviesa you can see the pimple of Cerrajon de Murtas the other notable peak of the Contraviesa and further to the east the Sierra de Gador in Almería.

6. At the two concrete water stores turn hairpin right to follow the track more or less on the contour into the *barranco*. After about 0.5km the track curves around the *barranco* and heads east, gently climbing.

   Ignore two minor tracks to the left.

7. At a chain across the track, ignore the sign prohibiting entry which relates to a disused quarry. Just past the chain take the left fork and follow the track as it descends a little to round a *barranco* and 300 or 400 metres later arrives at a hairpin bend where a minor track continues straight on.

   The route follows the main track downhill but if you are short of water there is a spring about 50m along the minor branch.

   Follow the main track down two hairpins and a few hundred metres later there is a holm oak to write home about and I do it the honour of giving it a number on the sketch map (8). It deserves more.

   In and around the Rambla de Torvizcón there are many scattered holm oaks, remnants of the original vegetation of these hills before man took a hand. The wood of these trees was particularly sought after as props for mining, it being resistant to rot in damp underground conditions and also for firing smelting furnaces in the form of wood or charcoal. Charcoal production was a big industry while the need and the trees lasted. At least a few remain and they are magnificent like that at (8). What an idea it would be to re-seed the hills with oak, cultivate "wild" boar to supply the ham-curers with local legs. All we need is an investor prepared to take a 50-year view.

   At point (8) a branch path leaves the track to the right and leads back to the cork oak forest as shown by the sketch map. The first few metres of this path are often lost by ploughing, but the path is there, entering the scrub about 10m above the oak.

8. After the oak the track bends downhill and 100m later arrives at a track junction.

9. Keep left at the junction.

   Ignore two minor tracks branching left, uphill and enter a patch of holm oaks in a *barranco*. Ignore a track branching right.

   The track makes three or four bends zigzagging downhill eastwards towards the valley bottom. On the last of these bends ignore a left turn which continues off to the north.

   Follow the main track as it heads south east now, passing first a *cortijo* on the left, then a ruin on the right then another large *cortijo* on the left. These *cortijos* are known as *Los Cerezillos*.

10. The track crosses the Rambla de Torvizcón. Route finding is easy from here. Follow the most obviously used track, always up and it arrives at the main road after about 3km, passing through almond and fig plantations and vineyards.

    Venta El Chaparro at (11) is too good a chance to miss for refreshment. As a wine and ham producer it seems a good place to try both. Its restaurant is a little more refined than many, well furnished, comfortable and quiet. The vino joven produced here isn't my favourite but try it. El Chaparro adds no black grapes to the pressing so the wine is without the pink colour. They make an excellent sweet wine from raisins of their own which if you like that sort of thing is worth the effort of carting home.

11. Turn right along the main road and after 2km, arrive at a road junction signed to Alfornón.

12. At this road junction two tracks branch off to the left through the vines. Take the steeper of the two, which follows the edge of the vines.

    At the top of the hill the vague track diverges in amongst the oaks, and later comes to a slightly isolated oak acting like a traffic island in the track junction. Take the lesser of the tracks straight on and follow it as it deteriorates and joins another well-made track. Turn right and follow the track to the main road. Turn left. Haza de Lino is in sight.

Walk 24. Juviles, Timar

A short walk, long on legend, history and interest. If it is not too hot the walk can be spun out to last all day by picnicking on top of El Fuerte. There is no shade there but it's a great place to enjoy the sun early or late in the year. Those relying on public bus for transport will have to take advantage of one or another of the bars offering accommodation in Juviles.

Time: 3 to 5 hours, more for serious dawdlers and picnickers.

Waymarks: The route joins the GR7 at Timar cemetery and follows it back to Juviles. Red and white painted posts and finger posts may be seen.

Difficulties: No water except in the villages. Between points (5) and (6) the path is little used and tends to get overgrown. There are one or two very short sections where the path is steep and eroded. They are not a serious problem if you have a stick or use the 'bottom shuffle' method.

Giants are not that common but take care on this walk; they are said to visit Juviles occasionally to look for one of their number who used to live here, in a vast cave under the limestone to the south east of the village.

Like us, giants are subject to the stresses of life and this one during the course of a crisis had a gigantic tantrum. The result was that 'Chez Giant' was shattered; the cave was burst open, rocks and debris scattered far and wide, and our maddened friend stamped off to pastures new.

His descendants, like all Spaniards have very strong links with their roots and come back to visit from time to time, which is why I suggest that you look around 'Chez Giant' carefully and with respect.

What you will see remaining of this ancestral home are three rocky outcrops rising about 20m above the surrounding ground. Each has a sheer face, one facing the other about 30m apart. These are of course the bases of internal pillars of the cave and on the south face of one can be seen the 2m imprint of a tantrum maddened foot. By my calculations a 2m foot makes the giant well, oh fee fi fo um ... quite big.

1. On exiting the village at its northern end, take c. Escuela, the side road passing around to the rear of the palatial ham drying warehouse.

   Turn right at the shop and keep tending to the right.

   Pass two turns to the right which head back into the village.

   The road deteriorates to a track and leaves the village. Where the concrete ceases, ignore a branch track leaving to the left.

2. 50m after the last buildings the track makes a right-angle bend to the right before continuing steeply down.

   From the bend at (2) is a good place to stop to get the idea of the three outcrops of rock that I like to call the pillars of Chez Giant.

   Where the track branches take the right option and follow it as it deteriorates and reverts to its original state of cobbled mule path. It descends by a set of tight zigzags.

   Part- way down a second set of zigzags, after a short straight section is a large holm oak on the left of the path (3). It is splitting the rock with its expanding roots. This holm oak serves to identify a minor access path to Chez Giant which leaves to the left. It leads via a minor *acequia* to a flat patch of land between two cliffs. La *Pisada* Del *Gigante* is part way up the south facing cliff.

   If the owner is about it is probably best to explain that you are looking for [La pis-<u>ath</u>-a del I-<u>gan</u>-tay]. If he is over 12 feet tall be especially polite.

   Perhaps having a sense of heritage a recent owner of this land, now sadly dead, has cared for it in a rather eccentric way. Is there something in the soil here that makes its owners different? He planted hundreds of vines around the site which are now doing their best in inhospitable conditions to grow up and over the cliffs. On top of one of the "pillars" he also planted a cypress complete with its own aerial irrigation pipe. All this being done for no reason other than the best one of all; for the pleasure of doing it.

   I hope the new owner catches the disease and that with his care, when you visit, 'Chez Giant' will be re-roofed with eccentric vines.

3. From the holm oak continue down the zigzags of the cobbled path. There is a relatively straight and level section passing the southern pillar of Chez Giant and its covering of vines and a small ruin on the right. It then zigzags to the south and passes an *alberca* on the left.

   Passing now to the west through olive and other fruit trees, the path arrives at a painted *cortijo* at (4).

4. The path hairpins right down among the poplars in the *barranco* but does not cross it.

   Pass a tiny white *casa de campo* on the left. Zigzagging down sometimes south, sometimes east, the path emerges from a rather overgrown section onto a small open terrace (5), with the cliff of El Fuerte close ahead to the east. A path branches right to cross the *barranco* to the west. This is the most obvious path but only leads to a field.

   The route is now at its least obvious but can be found passing down from one terrace to another. Looking over the treetops

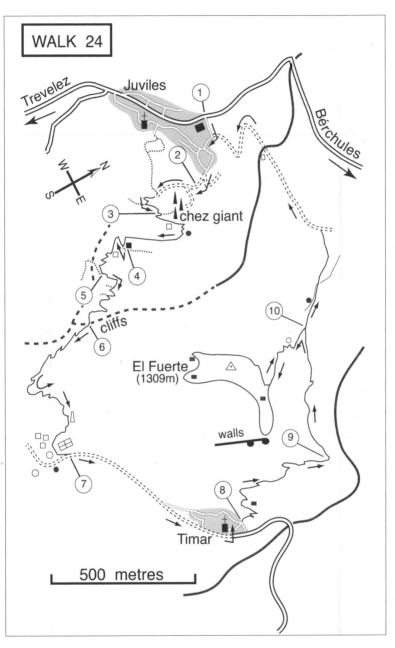

WALK 24

Trevelez
Juviles
①
Bérchules

W N
S E

②

③ chez giant

④

⑤

cliffs

⑥

El Fuerte
(1309m)

⑩

walls
⑨

⑦

⑧

Timar

500 metres

below, the path can be seen clearly skirting around the base of the cliff at the south end of El Fuerte.

5. If facing the cliff while standing on the terrace a path can be found on the right going down to the terrace below.

Go left from this terrace down to the one below. There now appears to be no way ahead but a path does lead down, south, towards the clear flat terrace immediately above the dense patch of trees in the cleft below. This patch contains three noticeably large boulders.

6. After zigzagging down to these boulders the path is at the very bottom of the cliff and then crosses the *barranco* to the left and emerges onto the clear path noticed from (5).

   Before rounding the southern cliff of El Fuerte don't forget to take a look back at the way you have come. A deep green gully, of great contrast to the terrain now entered, leads the gaze up to the skyline where the remains of Chez Giant are silhouetted.

7. The path arrives at Timar cemetery via the chimney, then turns left up the track towards the village.

   At (7) there is a strange mixture of things to see. The cemetery itself is interesting in demonstration the typical way burials are handled. The cemetery is almost always well out of the village and separate from the church. Most of the 'graves' are stacked pigeon holes into which coffins are slotted then sealed in.

   The era here is different from any other passed in the walks. Because the local stone here is limestone, rather than flat slate slabs, that has been used instead and more intricate patterns have resulted.

   If it is still there when you visit, the machine in the shed on the era is for winnowing. This hand-operated wind making and sieving device is the best I have seen, still in working order it may yet be in use but should be destined for a museum. It won't be surprising if it has gone by the time you visit.

   The remains of the mercury mining industry are rather unexpected. A chain of smelting chambers leading to the chimney can be seen and the dark red soil heap below the buildings is the spoil. Mercury has been mined in the area since Roman times. This is not the only mercury mine in the area, all are now abandoned.

   Follow the track into Timar keeping to the lower dirt road, ignoring the concrete left fork. Fill up with water in the plaza near the church then meander by any route up to the top of the village.

8. The path leaves the village from its top right corner, north east, following the GR7 to Juviles. It passes a water store building and zigzags up and across the east flank of El Fuerte which is now to the left of the path. Follow the most obvious path ignoring any minor deviations to the left.

9. Where the path stops climbing and begins to skirt the north face of El Fuerte is a good place to stop rest and look around carefully at

the canyon below. The path continues more or less on the contour, well defined, at the foot of the natural defences of El Fuerte.

The path crosses an eroded area of dusty grey soil. I say dusty assuming that it is dry, but it is the property of this soil when damp that make it worth mentioning. This is *launa*, the broken down product of the prevalent shaley mica rock.

It is this soil that has traditionally been used as the covering for the flat roofs that are a feature of Alpujarran architecture. When damp the dust transforms into a clay-like consistency, which is to a large extent impervious. As the owner of a house roofed with *launa* one has to constantly check that birds, mice etc. haven't dug holes in the surface, and every few years add another layer of *launa* to replace that which washes off in the rains. One also hopes not to have heavy rain on a dry roof; dry *launa* is not at all waterproof. Beneath the 2cm deep layer of *launa* there will be approximately 10cm of other soil to act as insulator and backup sponge. Under this either bamboo or large flat stones supported on the main beams of poplar or chestnut about 30cm apart.

10. Take the path, hairpin left which ascends to the top of El Fuerte. This normally has a wooden finger post pointing the way but in the absence of this it is quite an obvious path and it branches off left just before the main path begins to run alongside a concrete-channelled *acequia*.

El Fuerte is now, at first glance a barren hilltop but look around a bit and there are things to see. Lots of pottery and three *aljibes*, one with its domed roof missing and another complete, unexcavated and almost buried, these on the south tip of the site. Walking around the contour from the south to the east you pass another *aljibe* which looks as though a hermit took up residence from the number of carved crosses. Continue to the eastern corner to a point where you can look down on the rooftops of Timar and you are probably standing on the remains of a defensive wall, 1.5m wide which runs up and down the hill with tower bases at intervals. A lot of imagination is required to build it up to what it was over 1000 years ago; an eight-towered citadel.

Descend from El Fuerte by the same route, join the main path again and turn left. After 100m there is usually a wet section of

path and just to the left here is a naturalised *alberca* where a careful approach might be rewarded by some interesting sightings.

Cross the concrete channelled *acequia* and continue along the obvious path. Juviles is now coming into sight.

The path becomes a track, continue following it as it crosses a stream and continues up to the first village buildings.

At the buildings turn right to reach the main road.

Fuerte means strong. In the context of El Fuerte of Juviles it means fortress and it is fun to be able to link humble Juviles, by some history and a fair bit of imagination to the affairs of a great empire of the 8th century.

In amongst this hazy history a coup d'etat took place in Damascus, the centre of an expanding Syrian empire. The coup gave rise to a feud between the Nazrid and ousted Omeyan families. In an apparent attempt to pacify affairs, a great banquet of reconciliation was organised at which all members of the ousted family were killed; bar one. The sceptical Abd-Al-Rahman, having failed to convince his family of the danger had exiled himself rather than partake of poisoned sweetmeats.

In 755 he arrived in Almuñecar on the Granadan coast and made short work of establishing himself as emir in Córdoba, capital of the fledgling Muslim state of Al-Andalus. Al-Andalus was by no means a unified state, among the areas of independent and rebellious spirit was the Alpujurra where Moors and allied Pre-Moorish mozarabes set about defending the area with half a dozen castles, Juviles among them. They preferred to ally themselves with the new leadership in Damascus where they saw the real power.

Juviles castle came to be the strongest in The Alpujarra with a defensive wall and eight towers on top of the obvious natural defences.

130 years after the above events the rebellious spirit of The Alpujarra and other allied regions became too much for the dignity of the now Caliphate of Córdoba to bear. The caliph, non other than the grandson of the sceptical Abd-Al-Rahman mounted a military campaign to put an end to this insubordination. In 890 his army failed to subdue Juviles after a bloody battle, withdrew, but returned in 913. With previous experience of the problems and by mounting artillery on huge platforms the castle was eventually taken, the defenders suffering their fate.

Granada City

Fact File

Buses: It is possible to visit Granada from The Alpujarra by public bus, but it will take at least 4 hours out of the day and require an early start. (timetables in Appendix A). A taxi/bus is also needed from the out of centre bus station to the city centre.

City shuttle Buses: A good way to get a quick introduction to the city centre layout. Details in Appendix A.

Taxis: If short of time or energy use them. In a compact city they are not extravagant.

Driving to the city: It takes about 1hr 15min to drive from the western Alpujarra to Granada. For the stranger in town it is not worthwhile trying to drive in the city centre. Parking all day in the official Alhambra car park is reasonably priced. The easiest route is to follow Sierra Nevada/Alhambra signs from the motorway. After the tunnel follow Cemetery/Alhambra signs. This route, as far as exiting from the tunnel, is also valid for the suggested Hostal Suecia.

Accommodation: See Appendix B for some quiet and relatively convenient options.

The Alhambra

If visiting Granada for only one day, the reason is probably to visit the Alhambra. If this is the case, don't plan to do anything more than this. Rucksacks are not allowed into the monument but there is a left-luggage facility alongside the public toilets underneath the ticket office.

Alhambra tickets are limited to a fixed number for any morning or afternoon; they can become sold out. Advance booking is essential to avoid a possibly wasted visit. Tickets are bookable up to a year ahead by telephone (+34 90222 4460) or on www. alhambratickets.com. A reference number is given and tickets are collected at a special window with the minimum of queuing. Look for the word 'Anticipadas' over the window.

The Alhambra site is divided into three parts with three separate turnstiles, the ticket is valid either for morning (up to 2pm) or after-noon (after 2pm). Inside this period the portion of ticket valid for entry to the palace section has a specific ½ hr slot when entry must be made. This ½ hr time slot is chosen on making the advance booking. A leisurely visit to the palace takes about 2 hours, or for ever if you have a deep interest. Entry to the *Generalife* section (summer palace and water gardens) and the *Alcazaba* (fortress) can be made at anytime during the am or pm validity of the ticket. To avoid crowds, early morning or late afternoon are best but the problem cannot be entirely solved.

The Walks

The routes suggested will be of interest to those who are spending a night or more in the city and have time to browse rather than 'do'. The routes aim for ambience rather than monuments, but inevitably they are passed and the opportunities may be taken or ignored. It is assumed that the walks will be done during daylight.

In hot weather Granada is hotter than The Alpujarra, in cold, it is colder. While we as tourists will always be recognisable as such, we will blend better in some of the establishments mentioned if we leave off the Bermuda shorts and palm tree shirts and if possible leave the rucksack in the hotel.

Patio del Mexuar in the Alhambra

Walk 25. A Bit of City Life

Following this route gives the chance to watch the city going about its business, flowing in and out of bars, cafés and places of work. It incidentally passes by: the cathedral (closed 13.30 to 15.30), Capilla Real (closed 13.30 to 15.30), La Madraza, Monasterío De San Jerónimo (closes at 13.30) and Corral de Carbón (where there is a tourist information office). The opportunity therefore exists to visit, peep at or ignore any of these.

Time: From 2 hours upwards

---

1. Starting from Plaza Nueva, leave in the direction of c. Elvira (W) but turn left, just as leaving the plaza, into the streets of Hermosa, Silleria, Almireceros, Costa and Abenamar. These streets lead through to the busy thoroughfare Gran Via de Colon.

Work slowly through there streets concentrating on which bar, café or bodega might be to your taste either now or for later on in the day. Look out for Bodega La Mancha with the fancy wooden frontage. This is a good place for experimenting with wines and tapas. Tapas are charged for but the list is clear and easy to choose from.

2. Having crossed Gran Via de Colon you will be in sight of the cathedral. Go down c. Oficios where the Capilla Real and La Madraza face each other.

The cathedral and the Capilla Real are in fact part of the same building, have separate entrances and separate charges. If forced to choose, the Capilla Real is more interesting. If the guide books are anything to go by Granada is dominated by its Moorish fortress and palace but in all other respects it seems to emphasise its Catholicism. This came about in an Evangelistic frenzy at the beginning of the 16th century with the arrival in Granada of the Catholic conquistadores, Ferdinand and Isabela who are, or were, national heroes for sweeping the remains of Islam out of Spain.

The Capilla Real is the last resting place and shrine to the "Catholic Kings" and some of their family.

The redevelopment of the city in the 16th century, particularly with regard to public and religious buildings opened the way for the renaissance style; few Moorish-built buildings remain. One that does, faces the Capilla Real; La Madraza (Koranic school) survives from the 14th century but hugely renovated and altered down the years. One small part that remains intact from that time is the oratory, easily peeped at, just inside the main entrance from the street.

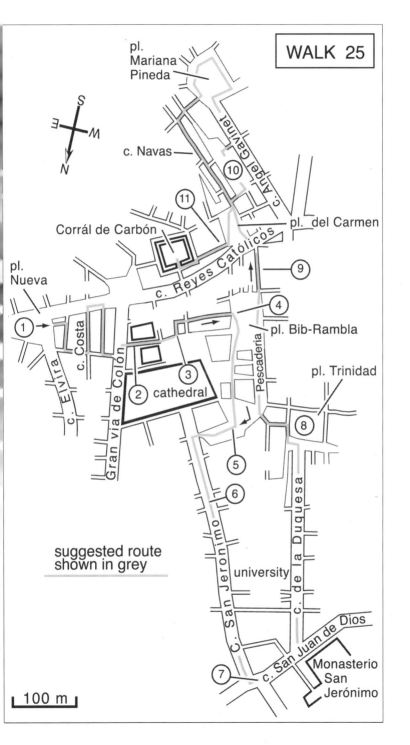

pl. Mariana Pineda

WALK 25

c. Navas

⑩

⑪

Corrál de Carbón

pl. del Carmen

c. Reyes Católicos

c. Angel Ganivet

pl. Nueva

⑨

①→

c. Costa

c. Elvira

④

pl. Bib-Rambla

③

② cathedral

Gran via de Colón

pl. Trinidad

Pescaderia

⑧

⑤

⑥

suggested route shown in grey

C. San Jerónimo

university

C. de la Duquesa

⑦

c. San Juan de Dios

Monasterio San Jerónimo

|_ 100 m _|

3. Continue down c. Oficios and delve off, left into a maze of knick-knack shops, the *Alcaicería* or silk market.

   The silk of The Alpujarra was big business and was traded world wide. The *Alcaicería* of today needs to be imagined along with c. Zacatín and other surrounding streets as a sort of Covent Garden of silk. It backed onto the river (which now flows under the streets Reyes Católicos and Acera de Darro) and a bridge linked it to *Corral de Carbón* on the opposite bank. It was a state controlled market, the authorities taking their share of taxes from the trade that passed through it.

   In a city that was changing hugely in the 19th century it is odd that after a fire in 1843 that totally destroyed the *Alcaicería* the area was rebuilt in replica, less the mosque and customs house that used to form part of this Mediaeval mall.

4. Emerge form the *Alcaicería* into Plaza Bib-Rambla which today devotes itself to eating, drinking and flowers but in earlier centuries was the centre for any significant event, be it jousting, bullfighting or politics. When leaving the square look for c. Colegio Catalino in the NE corner.

5. Enter the market area of Plaza Romanilla and passing through it, to the right arrive at c. San Jerónimo.

6. c. San Jerónimo runs north west from the cathedral past the university buildings and on to join c. San Juan de Dios.

   The university of Granada was founded by the Emperor Carlos V in 1526 and originally had its seat next to the archbishops palace, but has occupied the former Jesuit college in c. San Jerónimo since 1759. It was founded with five chairs, four of which were in theology and canon law, a sort of Catholic Madraza.

7. Turn left into c. San Juan de Dios and left again into c. de la Duquesa which leads to Plaza Trinidad.

   The patios and church of the Monasterío de San Jerónimo are accessible examples of how renaissance architects and artists, seeing Granada as a clean slate, set about building to the glory of God almost before the Muslims had been shown the gate. This particular building was started in 1496 under the patronage of the conquering royals, four years after taking power. Although not perhaps to modern taste it remains spectacular work despite the ravages of time.

   The 18th century was a bad time for San Jerónimo; Napoleon's troops did a nice line in looting and then the frescoes were applied which seem to detract, in the way of graffiti, rather than decorate.

8. From plaza Trinidad take c. Capuchinas, then turn right along c. Pescadería to enter plaza Bib-Rambla again.

A gate of similar construction to *Puerta de la Justicia* (see Walk 27) used to be on the site of No 8 in c. Capuchinas. This and another in plaza Bib-Rambla pierced the city wall that delimited the Moorish city.

The gate in plaza Bib-Rambla survived until 1884 when it was called *Puerta de las Orejas* after the customary hanging of ears from it after justice had been done. How fashions change; it was called *Puerta de las manos* (hands) in the 16th century.

9. Leave plaza Bib-Rambla by its South corner through c. Salamanca and cross the c. Reyes Católicos to plaza del Carmen where the town hall is.

10. Work through the block of streets delimited by plaza del Carmen, plaza Mariana Pineda and the c. Navas and Angel Garinet to return eventually to the town hall in plaza del Carmen.

the streets in the block from the town hall to plaza Mariana Pineda give a chance to mingle with the city folk going about their business. Their business often seems to involve visiting some fairly sophisticated bars and cafés for a quick one, or for a long lunch. I see no reason why we should not try to emulate them. Calle Navas is a good hunting ground for a drink or meal and around plaza Mariana Pineda are some economical eating places.

11. Leave the town hall plaza by c. Mariana Pineda, parallel to c. Reyes Católicos, then take the next right to find the Corrál de Carbón.

The original name for the *Corral de Carbón* was Alhóndiga Yidida. Alhóndiga being from the Arabic for caravanserai and Yidida after the name of the bridge (Alcántara Yidida = new bridge) by which it communicated with the commercial centre on the other side of the river (c. Reyes Católicos). It would have functioned as a lodging of last resort for travelling merchants, their stock and animals who could not find better hospitality. The portal with its Koramic inscriptions leads to two small vestibules from where the landlord controlled matters. A chaos of livestock would occupy the patio and the many small rooms surrounding the galleries would house the guests and their merchandise.

Well-constructed at the beginning of the 14th century from simple materials of brick, wood and plaster it has survived well without significant change or restoration. There were three other known Alhóndigas scattered through the commercial centre of the Moorish city but these have not survived.

Walk 26. The Albaicín

The Albaicín is the part of Granada with the longest history, excavations brought to light evidence of a town on this hilltop site from the 3rd century BC, through the Roman and Muslim eras to the present. The Alhambra palace and fortress is that constructed by the last dynasty of Muslims. Two other earlier dynasties chose the Albaicín site for their seats and some very early remains are visible today. The hill is a maze of narrow streets and blind alleys typical of Spanish Arab towns. It is easy to wander aimlessly and enjoy many little features on the way. This walk suggests a route taking in some of the charm and interest of the *barrio* but it is by no means the definitive or all-inclusive one. From the point of view of the views south across to the Alhambra and the Sierra Nevada it is best to be at the main view points late in the afternoon when the light is at its better angle.

Time: It depends on your interests but I suggest mid-morning through lunch to evening.

Note: The shuttle buses nos 31 and 32 pass points (17), (18) and (19) as well as plaza San Miguel Bajo, between (8) and (9).

1. Start at plaza Nueva and head up alongside the river.

2. Go left into Cuesta Santa Inés, then after passing the hotel go right, into c. Carnero. Turn left through placeta de la Concepción.

    Leave placeta de la Concepción by turning right into c. San Juan de los Reyes.

3. 50m later go left up the steps. Keeping to the steps and bearing left enter placeta Cobertizo.

4. Leave the *placeta* from its lower left corner and go along the level c. Rosal. Passing various turns left and right, pass through two small *plazas* to the end of c. Rosal at placeta Capellanes. Retrace steps to placeta Carrajales

5. Go down the steps from pl. Carrajales and right. Following this more or less level street leads through placeta Santa Inés Alta and then, to the right, placeta de Porras (6).

    The *Casa de Porras* in the square of the same name is a classy 16th-century house typical of many built at the beginning of the Christian era, using local Moorish skills. The style became known as Mudéjar. It is owned by the university, one may wander in and continue upstairs to the upper galleries. There is an *aljibe* under the central well head and a *carmen* to which we can't get access.

6. From the placeta de Porras go up the steps and right into cuesta de San Gregorio. Continue to placeta Cruz Verde where there is a *pensión* (see Appendix B).

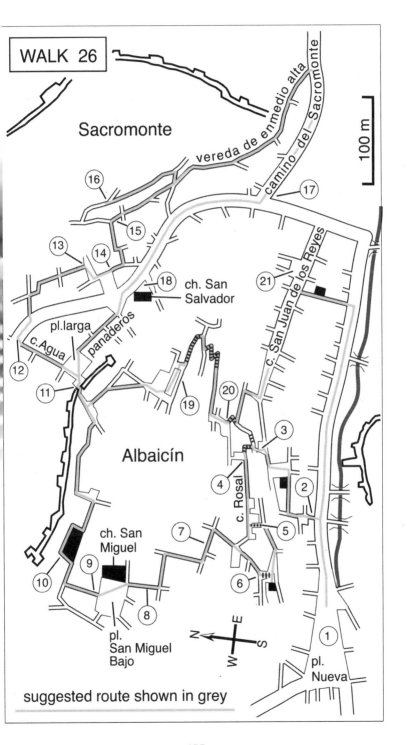

WALK 26

Sacromonte

vereda de enmedio alta

camino del Sacromonte

100 m

Albaicín

pl.larga

c.Agua

panaderos

ch. San Salvador

c. San Juan de los Reyes

c. Rosal

ch. San Miguel

pl. San Miguel Bajo

pl. Nueva

suggested route shown in grey

Continue up and pass c. Aljibe de Trillo on the right, then turn left into Muladar Doña Sancha (7).

Go right into c. de la Tiña. Go left into c. Clavel San José and right into c. Oidores, 'the street of listeners'.

8. c. Oidores leads into pl. San Miguel Bajo.

The pl. San Miguel Bajo is a pleasant place to take a break. If the church is open it is well worth a look at. From inside it is possible to see into the *aljibe* which was part of the ablutions court of the pre-existing mosque.

9. Take cjon. Gallo to cjon. De las Monjas.

In cjon. de las Monjas is the Palacio Daralhorra (open Monday, Wednesday and Saturday). The palace is the only Moorish building apart from the Alhambra, which is open to the public. It is also the most modern, constructed in the last few years of the reign of King Boabdil for his mother. Queen Isabel of Castile took it over as hers when she and Ferdinand of Aragon took the city over in 1492.

The building remains more or less intact and without reconstruction especially in its upper floors where close examination of the intricate decorated wooden ceilings is possible. The large timbers around the patio bear the original and fading Koranic inscriptions.

10. Turn right on leaving the Palacio Doralhorra. Keeping close to the old town walls, follow the road left through the Puerta de las Pesas. (11).

The section of town wall of which Puerta de las Pesas forms part is the earliest left visible in Granada. This 11th-century defence for the then town of Elvira replaced a smaller one destroyed by earlier power struggles. The visible holes in the wall are evidence of the method of construction: the paddling of earth and stone between shuttering of wood. When the wall had dried, the poles securing the shuttering were withdrawn, leaving holes, and the shuttering moved on to the next section. Excavations at the base of this wall have revealed remains of earlier ones dated at 300 BC constructed by Iberian inhabitants as well as later Roman constructions. The Puerta de las Pesas (The gate of weights) is so called because of the custom of hanging inaccurate, false weights from it, perhaps along with their users.

11. Passing through the gate leads to the plaza Larga, centre of the Albaicín's commercial life.

There is a good feeling of busy village life around c. Aqua and pl. Larga, with all the ordinary shops providing staple products for local residents and very little pandering to tourists. Saturday market provides a particularly chaotic scene

From plaza Larga follow c. Aqua to its junction with c. Pages.

12. Turn right into c. Pages and next left into placeta de las Estrellas. Next right into c. Cuestacilla and straight on into Callejon Mentidero.

There is an interesting blind alley opposite where c. Aqua joins c. Pages. Calle Cuestacilla offers a nice glance over gardens, and the Generalife to the Sierra Nevada. Calle Mentidero and placeta Mentidero are street names found in nearly every town and village. The place where people habitually gathered to talk, tell stories, plot and plan, and make speeches, came to be called the *mentidero*, a sort of speaker's corner, literally translated it means a place to tell lies.

13. Turn right out of c. Mentidero and left into Buenaventura which leads through plaza del Aliatar.

Just opposite pl del Aliatar is pl del San Salvador (18) to which the route returns later after the brief exploration of the Sacromonte barrio below. Sacromonte is known as the gypsy quarter. The hill above the last of the houses in c. Cruz de la Rauda is open country of prickly pear and agave vegetation, dotted with caves both inhabited and deserted. The houses in c. Cruz de la Rauda and c. de San Luis (which continues as Vereda Enmedio) though with traditional frontages are caves internally. The area as a whole will appeal to those with an interest in gypsy culture, flamenco and zambra music and dance. It is easy to find establishments where concerts and shows are advertised.

14. Leave pl. del Aliatar by c. Buenaventura.

Take the left turn opposite Carmen Patricia.

Keep left to pass by Carmen de San Raphael and join c. de San Luis (15), the larger street running along the contour at the end of the alley.

Look out for c. Cueras Coloradas on the left, turn into it and left gain into c. Cruz de la Rauda (16).

Arriving at the cross there is a fine view which includes all the roofs of the Albaicín, the valley of Río Darro, the Alhambra and the distant Sierra Nevada. The cross itself is a nice old piece of work from the 16th century. It was destroyed in 1932 when anarchistic rioting celebrated the separation of church from state during the second republic. Using some of the original parts the cross was reconstructed in 1936 when the political pendulum began to swing back with a vengeance. Rauda is from an Arabic word meaning cemetery. This area was a burial site during the Moorish era.

16. From the cross, retrace your steps back to c. de San Luis and turn left following the road along the contour. It is variously named: Chinos and Vereda de Enmedio Alta.

The section of old city walk that is passed here is contemporary with the Alhambra, about 300 years younger than the walls near the plaza Larga. A little further on from the wall and fuente amapola is a tiny cave bar which provides a good excuse to sit and enjoy yet another view and beer.

Continue on, and taking any right turn, gradually descend to the car access road, Camino del Sacromonte. Turn right and follow this main road back towards the Albaicín.

17. Turn right at Peso de la Harina, uphill and follow the road as it leads to the church of San Salvador in pl. San Salvador.

A few minutes spent in the church of San Salvador are worthwhile. This was the site of the main mosque of Muslim Albaicín, the patio and the arcades remain from that period. The church itself has had a turbulent time; during its first 50 years it was almost destroyed by Muslim rebels of the 16th century and recently in the 1936 war by left and anarchist factions.

18. Turning left out of the church of San Salvador leads to c. Panaderos and this in turn to pl. Larga.

Pass again through Puerta de las Peseas (11), left into cjon. De San Cecilio and thus into the large square, at the far end of which is the church of San Nicolás and the more famous viewpoint (to which any taxi will take you), Mirador de San Nicolás.

The Mirador de San Nicolás is regarded as the point from which to view the Alhambra at its best. It may be. As a photographer, you will find the subject much easier late in the day or even at dusk or sunset.

The aljibe here is one of the most easily viewed in that its dome is above ground level although even then most of the structure is below ground. (See walks 9 and 24, aljibes in more rustic settings).

19. Some steps lead down and left from the Mirador de San Nicolás. Cuesta de las Cabras.

At the bottom of the steps cross the road near Aljibe de las Tomases and down the steps of Cuesta de las Tomases.

Continue down to placeta Aljibe de Trillo where there is a restaurant.

20. Take the steps down to the left of the restaurant's door. Half-way down the steps take the level street on the left c. Limón.

Turn right at the first opportunity, placeta Escuelas, to join c. San Juan de los Reyes, the level car-access street. Turn left.

Walking along San Juan de las Reyes is one of the highlights of an Albaicín stroll. Every glance down every side street provides a memorable snap-shot. The sepia colouring of tiles and stone helping to age the views out of the present and assisting the imagination into a little bit of time-travelling escapism.

Continue along San Juan de los Reyes as far as placeta Victoria.

21. Retrace steps a few metres from pl. Victoria then turn left down c. Horno de Oro where there is another Moorish house sometimes open for viewing. Turn right alongside the river to return to the start point.

Walk 27. Around the Alhambra Hill

The walk involves climbing from the Río Darro to the highest point of the Alhambra site where the ticket office is and later a second climb from Campo Principe to Torres Bermejas. (16). It also provides lots of shade, bars with and without views, shady ornamental gardens and to end it all an armchair.

Time: There is too much in this walk to enjoy in one day. From point (5) onwards there are various sections that can be left out or not as your interest dictates. If for instance you are particularly interested in gardens leave (10) out and devote a morning to it specifically. The same would be true of the Alhambra site (6) to (9) if you are a museum and fine art fanatic.

Notes: The start point is Plaza Nueva but since the walk is circular join in wherever is convenient.

1. From Plaza Nueva head up Carrera del Darro (NE) and passing one bridge, (*Puente Cabrera*) cross to stand on the second (2).

   Looking up and down the course of the river from the bridge it doesn't take much imagination to visualise the city as it might have been before the river was buried under Plaza Nueva, Calle Reyes Católicos, Puerta Real and Acera del Darro. Thirteen bridges, like these visible, criss-crossed the river linking the two banks on average every 150m.

2. From *Puente* Espinosa return to Carrera del Darro and continue in the same direction as before. A wide esplanade opens out which is shared by the numerous bars which line the street.

   While recognising the attractions of sitting outside enjoying the sun and taking a little something under the Alhambra, bear in mind that the inside of a bar might have its own attractions, the waiter will be more amiable if he hasn't walked 50m to deliver your drink and also it will be cheaper inside. With this in mind bar Casa 1899 is a nice one to use.

3. Where the road makes a right angle bend and becomes Cuesta del Chapiz, turn right over the river bridge (*Puente* Rey Chico) and follow the cobbled road, Cuesta de Los Chinos. This leads to near the Alhambra ticket office.

   Cuesta de Los Chinos is a pleasant pedestrian path leading between the Alhambra and the Generalife. It is steep enough to lead us to take advantage, every few minutes, of the changing view back over the city. Near the top, the path passes under an aqueduct carrying the water that feeds the water-system of the Alhambra.

4. Soon after the aqueduct the path passes a restaurant and joins the road which gives taxi and bus access to the Alhambra site. Turn right down the hill to a point where a central path begins, opposite

the Hotel Washington Irving. Continue down the path to the first junction (5).

A choice exists at (5), to miss out a brief exploration of those parts of the Alhambra site that do not require a ticket. The suggested route will later return to this point.

5. Turn right and join the branch of the road which leads through Puerta de Los Carros (6).

6. Turn to the right and follow the road past the church of Santa Maria towards the Hotel Parador San Francisco (7).

The Hotel occupies the site of a Franciscan monastery that was founded here in 1495, three years after the expulsion of the Muslims. Nothing remains of it but the hotel offers a smart resting place while taking refreshment. The stairs to the left of reception lead down to a bar which has a terrace offering a unique spot from which to view the Generalife and rest quietly, while taking the worst and most expensive breakfast in Granada.

7. Return down the same road towards the Palacio de Carlos V (8).

The palace is thought to be a splendid example of Renaissance art to be compared with the best in the world but its siting has led others to vitriol. Compared with Carlos' plans, it stands unfinished which is probably just as well. Entry is free to European passport holders. It houses a fine art museum and a museum of artefacts found during the restoration of the Alhambra.

There's a nice story of the origins of the palace, based on love and cold nights. The Emperor Carlos V of Spain visited Granada in the summer of 1526 having recently married Isabel of Portugal. They lived in the Moorish palace of the Alhambra but as the summer stretched on to autumn the lack of modern facilities and the cold became too much for Isabel who took herself off to more comfortable lodgings in the Monasterío de San Jerónimo. Carlos attended to matters, shivered and sulked in the Alhambra until December. Having been bewitched by Granada and Isabel alike he commissioned the building of a modern palace to satisfy his two loves.

8. From the Palacio de Carlos V follow the signs to Puerta del Vino then turn down the roadway leading to Puerta de la Justicia (9).

Puerta de la Justicia is one of my favourite parts of the Alhambra, partly because we know it is in more or less its original state, also because of its materials and shapes. Constructed in 1348 its outer arches show the typical engravings of the key and hand, of Koranic significance. The magnificent door of cladded palm wood, its heavy smoothed iron fittings, and the brickwork in the tortuous passage make the Alhambra worthy of a visit for its sake alone.

9. From here follow the road back up the hill to (5).

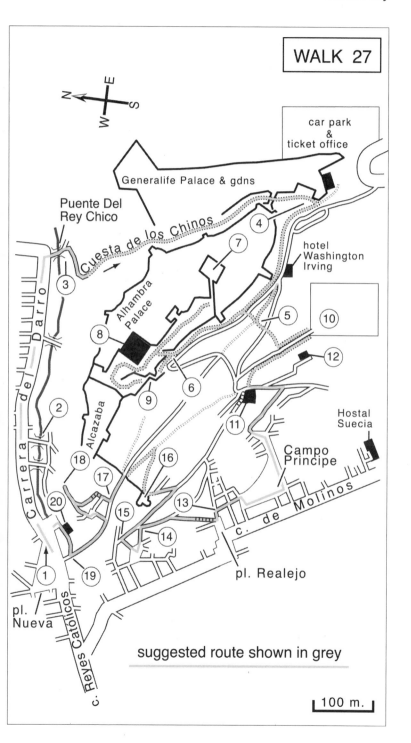

WALK 27

car park & ticket office

Generalife Palace & gdns

Puente Del Rey Chico

Cuesta de los Chinos

Alhambra Palace

Alcazaba

hotel Washington Irving

Campo Principe

Hostal Suecia

c. de Molinos

pl. Realejo

Carrera del Darro

pl. Nueva

c. Reyes Católicos

suggested route shown in grey

100 m.

161

5. Follow the sign indicating Carmen de los Martires. At the next junction of paths, turn left up to the entrance to the *carmen* (10).

The gardens offer a quiet interlude, somewhere to picnic, read a book or feed the ducks. Gardeners will be interested in the gardens which although all designed in the 19th century are intended to be French, Spanish and Arab in style as well as including areas of fruit, vegetables and herbs.

Carmen is a Granadan word meaning garden in either an urban or country house setting. Not an unusual concept in England, but unusual enough in Spain to have to coin a local word for it.

When the Christians took control of Granada they found silos on this site which some sources tell us had been used as prisons for captured Christian priests who were later executed. Hence the name Carmen de los Matires. It later became the site of a Carmelite convent with St John of the Cross as prior in 1582. During his incumbency he planted a "Mexican cedar" (cupressus lustitanica) which still presides over one of the upper gardens.

10. On leaving Carmen de los Martires follow the left-hand side of the road, past the iron gates and down the steps to the big pink, Alhambra Palace Hotel (11).

The hotel bar has a terrace, famous for its view of the city and the country beyond. Past reception and to the right.

11. Turn right on leaving the hotel. On the left is a small street, c. Matamoros, signed to *Casa Museo Manuel de Falla* (12).

12. This is worth a quick visit to see a more normal, smaller house and *carmen* that were the home of Granada's famous composer.

Continuing down the hill from the hotel, take the road, hairpin right that leads down to the church of San Cecilio.

Continue downhill to a large plaza, Campo Principe.

Campo Principe is a good place to arrive at with lunch in mind. There is plenty of choice and the clientele is more 'normal' and less 'tourist'. Don't be put off by the ridiculous décor of Restaurante La Infa, it has a good long menu and reasonable prices, a good variety of fish especially worthy of a try. (Don't get confused by there being a Hotel La Infa, also ridiculously decorated, at the opposite end of the plaza. Plaza Realejo (13) would also make a good lunch stop.

Leave from the north end of Campo Principe, past Hotel La Infa in ·c. Cocheras. Turn left into plaza Realejo.

13. From pl. Realejo, turn right into c. Damasceros and immediately right up the steps to pass alongside Carmen de Santa Catalina.

14. At the crossroads of Callejon Puerta del Sol, Allamillos and

Azacayuela Alta, turn left into Puerta del Sol and Placeta Berrocal, then right, out of Berrocal to meet c. Cruz de Piedra at (15).

Passing through this barrío which was the Jewish quarter of the Muslim city it is worth remembering that 1492 not only marked the end of Islam in Spain but also Judaism, in fact the inquisition sharpened their teeth on the Jews giving the Granadan Muslims time to see how the wind was blowing and exile themselves.

15. Turn right up c. Cruz de Piedra and follow the road, hairpin left leading to the mini-castle of Las Torres Bermejas (16).

Looking over the wall near the towers, alongside the gate into Carmen de San Antonio, gives a birds-eye view of the Medieval looking areas surrounding the modern plaza Nueva.

The largest tower of the Alcazaba, Torre Vela with its bell tower is at the western extreme of the Alhambra site. The bell's function was administrative rather that warning; it was used to control the irrigation system of the agricultural plain around the city. Even in rural Alpujarra, the Moorish municipalities had their boundaries based on water catchment areas and acequia networks. The bell controlled the opening and shutting times of sluices at specific times night and day to ensure every property got its legal share of water.

16. Turn down the cobbled path to the right of the towers. At the junction lower down, turn left. Pass under the arch on Cuesta de Gomerez.

17. 100m below the arch turn right into Almanzora Baja. After 50m turn right up the steps past the gate to Carmen Porredano. Continue, tending right and up along Almanzora Alta (18).

Almanzora Alta is a blind alley but gives sight down onto the many notable buildings lining pl Nueva and Río Darro. Across on the hill opposite is the Albaicín barrio.

From this viewpoint a spaciousness, provided by internal courtyards and walled carmens, is apparent; the opposite of the effect gained by walking the streets and alleys.

18. Retrace your steps through Almanzora Alta to the gate of Carmen Santo Domingo then left into placeta de la Miga. Go down and left to meet cuesta Gomerez again. Turn right.

19. Turn right 30m before it meets pl Nueva, into the street Hospital Santa Ana.

The bar Pilar del Toro (20) may be just the place you need; it has a bar room on the immediate right, ideal for a few drinks and a serious discussion or a domino session, a courtyard with armchairs for the tea and cake ceremony (the cheese cake – tarta de queso – is the best), and a restaurant. It was the armchair that sold it to me.

Appendices

Appendix A – Public Transport
Routes in Granada City
There are three mini-bus routes in Granada that shuttle around the main tourist areas. They are all circular routes giving the opportunity to get the lie of the city and spot places of interest at which to get off, next time round. None of the routes take more than 30min. No 32 is the best one for a general look around. For a group or for taking various journeys a *"bonobus"* ticket is cheaper and more convenient. Details are displayed on the buses.

Route 30 – Alhambra: shuttles between the Alhambra and Plaza Isabel la Católica.

Route 31 – Albaicín: circular route, Plaza Nueva, Albaicín, cathedral, plaza Nueva.

Route 32 – Alhambra/Albaicín Conexión: circular route combining 30 and 31

Taxis

Orgiva	958 785740	Office on street between petrol station and traffic lights. Car hire and taxi.
Capileira	958 763125	
Pitres	958 766055	Ask at the supermarket
Trevelez	958 858537	Ask in hardware shop (*ferretería*) Plaza Barrío Medio
Mecina Bombarón	958 851021	Ask at the shop between the town hall and the pharmacy
Juviles	616 035423	
Castaras	616 035423	

Buses to and from The Alpujarra
Times are liable to change but over recent years they have remained the same. The bus company is T. Alsina Graells Sur S.A. Their ticket offices are obvious in the bus stations and tickets can be bought on the bus where there are no ticket offices. The buses are red & white.

Route Malaga – Granada
Malaga bus station is served by a shuttle bus from the airport or a 15 minute taxi ride. Journey time Malaga – Granada: 2 hours.

Depart Malaga:
07.00 08.00 09.00 10.00 11.00 12.00
13.30 14.00 14.30 15.00 16.00 17.00 18.00
19.00 20.00 21.00 (22.00 Friday, Sunday and holidays)

Depart Granada:
07.00 08.00 09.00 09.30 10.00 11.00
12.00 13.00 13.30 15.00 16.00 17.00
18.00 19.00 20.00 21.00 (22.00 Friday, Sunday and holidays)

Route Malaga – Órgiva – Lanjarón

The only route from Malaga to The Alpujarra with no changes. Not Sundays or holidays.
Depart Malaga: 15.30
Depart Órgiva: 08.15; Arrive Malaga 11.45

Route Almería – Bérchules

A good alternative to going via Granada from Almería. One bus a day, no changes.
Depart Almería bus station: 15.45
Depart Bérchules: 06.00; Arrive 09.45

Route Granada – Pitres/Bérchules/Alcutar

Departure times from the termini are accurate but those of intermediate villages depend on conditions. Buses can pass up to 20 minutes early.

From Granada			Town	From The Alpujarra		
10.30	12.00	17.15	Granada	08.45	18.15	20.45
12.00	13.30	18.45	Órgiva	07.15	16.30	19.30
12.35	14.05	19.20	Pampaneira	06.30	16.00	18.30
12.55	14.25	19.40	Capileira	06.30	15.50	18.20
13.15	14.45	20.00	Pitres	06.00	15.30	18.00
	14.50	20.05	Pórtugos	05.50		17.50
	14.55	20.10	Busquístar	05.45		17.45
	15.15	20.30	Trevélez	05.30		17.30
	15.25	20.40	Puerto de Cástaras	05.20		17.20
	15.35	20.50	Juviles	05.15		17.15
	15.45	21.00	Bérchules	05.05		17.05
	15.50	21.05	Alcutar	05.00		17.00

Granada – Alpujarra (east) via Torvizcón, Puerto Juviléy, Mecina Bombarón, Yegen.

		Town		
08.30	18.00	Granada	09.30	20.15
10.15	19.50	Órgiva	07.45	18.15
10.40	20.10	Puerto Juviléy	07.15	17.40
10.50	20.20	Torvizcón	07.15	17.35
11.25	20.50	Cádiar	06.30	17.00
11.30	20.55	Mecina Bombarón	06.00	16.30
11.45	21.10	Yegen	05.45	16.15
12.30	22.00	Ugíjar	05.30	16.00

Appendix B – Accommodation

The accommodation list shows a selection only of those establishments recommended for one reason or another. Details are liable to
change and may not be complete.

Key

↝	H = Hotel; P = Pension; B&B = other; A = self-catering
$	Price band: L = Low; M = Medium; H = Higher
🍽	Meals (Y/N); 🌡 = Heating (Y/N)

Name	↝	$	🍽	🌡	Comment
Granada City					
Hostal Suecia, c. Molinos, Huerta de los Angeles, 8. Granada. 18009. Tel: 958 225044, 958 227781. Fax: 958 225044	P	M	N	Y	Relatively easy to drive to and park. Good leafy location. Cheap for city. Pleasant place
Casa del Aljarife, Placeta de la Cruz Verde, Albaicín. Granada. Tel/fax: 958 222425. www.granadainfo.com/most E-mail: most@wanadoo.es	P	H	N	Y	Beautiful house and location 5 minutes walk from the nearest parking. Reasonably priced for its location
Cuevas el Abanico, Sacromonte. Granada. www.el-abanico.com. Tel: 958 226 199	A	H	N	-	Something a bit different. 1- or 2-bedroomed modernised caves. Sacromonte/Albaicín location.
Camping					
Orgiva	-	-	Y	-	Camping and chalets
Pitres Tel: 958 766111. www.balcondepitres.com	-	-	Y	-	Camping and chalets
Trevelez Tel: 958 858735	-	-	Y	-	Camping and chalets

The Poqueira Valley

Name	↝	$	🍽	🌡	Comment
Pampaneira					
Hostal Pampaneira (Restaurante Alfonso) Tel: 958 763002, 958 763107	P	M	Y	Y	
Bubion					
Villa Turistica *** www.villabubion.com. Tel: 958 763909 Fax: 958 763905	H	H	Y	Y	Rooms or houses within the complex for two to six people.
Hostal las Terrazas, Plaza del Sol, Bubion. Tel: 958 763034	P A	L	N	Y	Breakfast only. Pleasant people, comfortable lounge, good value, quiet

Capileira

Finca Los Llanos *** c. Sierra, Capileira. Tel: 958 763071 Fax: 958 763206	H A	H	Y	Y	Rooms or apartments some single rooms closed in January/February for 4 weeks
Meson Poqueira c. Dr. Castilla, 11 Tel: 958 763048 Fax: 958 763048	P A	L	Y	Y	Rooms or apartments
Refugio Poqueira Tel: 958 343349	P	L	Y	-	Great facilities bearing in mind the location: refuge at 2500m on Mulhacen. Unisex, communal dormitory and washroom. Ask for sheets if you don't have a sleeping bag. Blankets provided.

La Taha de Pitres

Pitres

Hotel San Roque ** Tel: 958 857528 Fax: 958 857528	H	M	Y	Y	Very nice rooms, especially those at the front with a south view

Buquístar

Casa Sonia Tel/Fax: 958 857503 Email: sonia@teleline.es	B & B	M	N	Y	Lovely house, village centre location. Breakfast only. Good position for walking. English spoken.

Mecina

Hotel Albergue de Mecina www.hotelalberguedemecina. com Tel: 958 766254 Fax: 958 766255	H	H	Y	Y

Ferreirola

Sierra y Mar www.sierraymar.com Tel: 958 766171 Fax: 958 857367	B & B	M	N	Y	Beautiful situation, run by walkers. Breakfast only. Closed December and January

Trevelez

Hotel La Fragua * San Antonio, 4, Barrío Medio. Tel: 958 858626 Fax: 958 858614	H	M	Y	Y	Excellent restaurant under the hotel's management 50m away. Good situation. Closes January/February for 4 weeks
Alcazaba de Busquistor *** www.alpujarralcazaba.com Tel: 958 858687 Fax: 958 858693	H	H	Y	Y	The best facilities of any Alpujarran hotel, also the most expensive, but good value. 4km east of Trevelez, car essential

There are many other places to stay in Trevelez.

Bérchules

Hotel Las Bérchules **	H	M	Y	Y	Useful base for the eastern
Tel: 958 852530					Alpujarra. English spoken.
Fax: 958 769000					
Email:					
hot.berchules@interbook.net					
La Posada, Pl. de Abastos, 7	B	L	Y	-	Good village position.
Tel: 958 852530 or	&				Interesting traditional house
958 343320	B				

Hotel La Fragua, Trevelez

Mecina Bombarón

Casas Blancas www.casasblancas.turincon.com Email casasblancas@mundivia.es Tel: 958 851151	A	M	N	Y	Worth using if only to take advantage of the heated indoor pool. Houses in village for 2-6
Los Molinos **www.arrakis.es/~molinos**	A	H	N	Y	Well-restored mills in perfect location. Selfcatering. On walks 17-20

Yegen

El Rincon de Yegen Tel: 958 851270	P	M	Y	Y	On the road out to the east. Rooms or apartments. Good restaurant
Pension La Fuente Tel: 958 851067	P	L	Y	Y	Very good value. Friendly people.

Miscellaneous

Juviles

Bar Pension Tino Tel: 958 769174	P	L	Y	-	Slightly off the main road at the west end of the village.
Pension Fermandez Tel: 958 769030	P	L	-	-	Simple old house with charm. Cheap. Alongside vine-covered Bar Fernandez. I have a soft spot for this place; they once put an electric fire in my room when all the others let me shiver.

Cástaras

Pension Maria tel: 958 855547	P	L	-	-	Cheap and simple – on Walk 22. Knock on the door next to the normally shut Bar Maria.

Accommodation becomes limited at busy times of the year and it is worth booking ahead if visiting the area at the following periods: New year, Epiphany (January 6/7), February 28, Easter week, May 1, August, October 12, November 1, December 6, 7, 8.Individual villages become full at times of their fiestas:

Pampaneira	May 3, 4, 5
Bubión	January 20, August 20
Capileira	last week in April
Pitres	August 16, 17, 18
Trevélez	June 13, August 4/5, October 19/20
Juviles	January 20, October 20
Bérchules	April 25, 26, 27, July 27, August 10
Mecina Bombarón	November 28, 29, 30

Most of the dates move to the nearest weekend.

Appendix C – Glossary of Spanish terms

aceite [a-<u>they</u>-itay] – oil, in the food sense, olive oil is assumed

acequia [a-<u>thek</u>-eea] – a canal, man-made, to carry water to where it is needed for agricultural or domestic purposes. Originally simply hewn from earth or rock but increasingly of concrete or piped. In Moorish times the network of *acequias* in The Alpujarra reached 2,000km. It is estimated that 500km remain in use, less every year.

alberca [al-<u>bear</u>-ka] – a water reservoir, usually small, used to store irrigation water from *acequias* prior to use. May be a pit of earth and stone or concrete.

alcazaba [alkath-<u>ab</u>-ba] – fortress or castle. Also the name of a mountain peak in the Sierra Nevada.

aljibe [al-<u>he</u>-bay] – from the Arabic for water stone. A brick or masonry water store, usually built partially underground and with a domed roof. To store water from a nearby spring without it becoming contaminated or warm.

almendras [al-<u>men</u>-dras] – almonds.

artesa [ah-<u>tes</u>-a] – a large wooden trough with tapering sides and horizontal end boards. Used for hand-mixing large quantities of food as at a pig killing when mixing sausage or for kneading dough.

azotea [atho-<u>tay</u>-a] – a balcony or room on the upper floor of an Alpujarran house, open to the sides but roofed. Used for drying and storing foodstuffs.

baño [<u>ban</u>-yo] – bath. When on maps, medicinal baths, usually ruined.

barra [<u>ba</u>-rra] [ba] as in bat – the normal word for a loaf of bread

barranco [ba-<u>rank</u>-ko] – a water eroded feature of landscape. From valley size down to ditch size. May or may not have water flowing.

barrio [<u>ba</u>-rio] – a district within a village, town or city.

bco. – abbreviation of *barranco*

borreguil [borre-<u>geel</u>] – high mountain pasture briefly verdant in summer when snow has melted. Literally means sheep pasture. Of significance in summer when grass is short elsewhere.

calle [<u>ky</u>-yay] – street

callejón [ky-yeh-<u>hon</u>] – a little street, narrow or short.

camino [kam-<u>een</u>-o] – path or route

campesino [camp-eh-<u>seen</u>-o] – a worker on the land.

carbón [car-<u>bon</u>] – coal, charcoal

cárcel [<u>car</u>-thel] – prison.

careo [ka-<u>rayo</u>] – a word from north-west Spain meaning rough mountain terrain for grazing. Pasture.

carmelita [calm-e-<u>litre</u>] – carmelite

carmen [<u>car</u>-men] – from Arabic for vine, a Granadan word for garden.

casa [<u>kas</u>-a] – house

casa de campo [<u>kas</u>-a de <u>cam</u>-po] – a cross between a tool shed, a kitchen and a bedroom. A very small building set on a plot of land for storage and shelter.

castaño [ka-<u>stan</u>-yo] – sweet chestnut tree

cerezo [the-<u>reth</u>-o] – cherry tree

cerezillo [the-<u>reth</u>-eeyo] – little cherry tree

coco [<u>ko</u>-ko] – coconut (dulce de coco=macaroon)

corral [ko-<u>ral</u>] – corral

cortijo [kor-<u>tea</u>-ho] – house surrounded by its land where a family or families live or lived all or part of the year.

costa [<u>cost</u>-a] – coast, but in relation to wines it is the rosé wine of the Sierra de la Contraviesa, Granada.

crestones [crest-<u>tony</u>'s] – crest or sharp ridge

cuesta [<u>quest</u>-a] – hill, slope. Also cost.

culo [koo-low] – backside, arse.

dorado [do-<u>rarth</u>-oh] – golden

duende [<u>dwen</u>-day] – ghost, spirit, soul.

dulce [<u>dulth</u>-e] – sweet (adj.) or cake.

encina [en-<u>theen</u>-a] – *quercus ilex*, holm oak.

encinar [enthin-aah] – oak woods.

era [<u>err</u>-a] – sounds like 'error' – a circle of stone for threshing, winnowing and drying. Belongs to a nearby *cortijo* but perhaps sited away from it in a windy position.

estanco [es-<u>tank</u>-oh] – shop selling official forms, postage stamps etc. See also 'tabacos'.

ferreteria [ferret-air-<u>ee</u>-a] – hardware shop usually of the type where nothing you want is visible but it is there if you know how to ask for it.

fiesta [fee-<u>est</u>-a] – from a birthday party to weeks jollification. A day off. Usually associated with the firing off of enough gunpowder to supply a small war.

fragua [<u>frag</u>-wa] – forge

fria [<u>free</u>-a] – cold (adj.)

fuente [<u>fwen</u>-tay] – village fountain or spring of drinking water in any situation. Always drinkable unless the words "no *potable*" are displayed.

gigante [hig-<u>ante</u>] – giant (n.) (adj.)

gorda [<u>gourd</u>-a] – fat, round (f. adj.)

gordo [<u>gourd</u>-oh] – fat, round (m. adj.)

horno [<u>orn</u>-oh] – oven, in the sense used always a brick dome with external lime plastering, built either integral with the kitchen cooking fireplace, or external to the house. For bread-making primarily. Also the term used for a bakers shop where larger versions would be used. The normal domestic size is about 1 metre in diameter. A good one is visible on an *azotea* in the square at Atalbétar and a commercial one in the horno de Luisa, c. Horno, Capileira. (Walk 1)

isla [<u>is</u>-la] – island.

jamón [ham-<u>mon</u>] – ham. In The Alpujarra, assume *jamón serrano* – air-cured ham, literally from the *sierra*. Air conditions and the micro-flora existing in the Sierra Nevada enable the drying of ham without the injection of salts or preservatives and without cooking. Pig killings are traditionally timed for January or December to take advantage of the cool months when the ham is young. Ham is eaten after 12 or more months of drying. They have a layer of fat larded over them to protect them from surface infection while on display/drying. Curing is one of the most valuable businesses of The Alpujarra although the pigs are raised elsewhere.

laguna [la-<u>goon</u>-a] – tarn.

largo [<u>lar</u>-go] – long, big (adj.).

launa [<u>lown</u>-a] – 'lown' as in town. A grey earth used on flat roofs as waterproofing. A fine grey dust, the breakdown product of the grey slatey magnesium bearing rock common in the area. When damp the dust becomes clay-like in property. When saturated it forms a semi-fluid slime which as a seam through a hillside can cause sections of hills to slide down, roads to fall etc. Many bare areas are seen where vegetation never gets the opportunity to grow because of the easily eroded nature of launa. More launa is added to the roofs periodically to replace that which inevitably washes off in the rain.

medio [<u>med</u>-eeo] – half, for example – medio kilo. A useful word to use when a stall holder or shopkeeper is trying to sell you twice what you need. Barrío medio = the middle barrio.

menu [<u>men</u>-oo] – menu. Usually used in the sense of *menu del dia* – menu of the day (see introduction – food).

molino [mol-<u>een</u>-oh] – mill. The grain mills frequently seen in The Alpujarra are sited near water for their power. Olive mills are also encountered (Walk 22), they were originally mule-powered and had conical stones like those displayed in Mecina (illustration page 75).

Mulhacén [mull-a-<u>then</u>] – the peak of the Sierra Nevada 3,482m. Named after the penultimate Arab king of Granada (1466-1485), Abul-h-Hassan Ali known as Muley Hacen. He presided over a period of decadence and intra-family intrigue before his son succeeded him and finally handed Granada over to the Christians in 1491 (see chapter the Poqueira Valley).

negro [<u>neg</u>-grow] – black.

no [no] [as in knot] – not, no.

noche [<u>notch</u>-eh] – night, noche vieja = new years eve.

pan [pan] – a general term for bread but not much use when purchasing: "I want some bread" "Yes, what do you want?" (see food glossary page 6).

perro [<u>perr</u>-ro] – dog.

pisada [piss-<u>arth</u>-a] – footprint.

placeta [plath-<u>ett</u>-a] – a tiny square in a town or village.

plaza [<u>plath</u>-a] – a town square

posada [pos-<u>arth</u>-a] – inn. Originally for travellers trading or moving livestock.

potable [pot-<u>tab</u>-blay] – drinkable, usually in relation to water. Safe to drink.

prado [<u>prar</u>-though] – meadow, field, flat land.

puente [<u>pwen</u>-tay] – bridge over river etc. A long weekend, taking advantage of joining two official holidays.

ración [rath-ee-<u>on</u>] – food portion, a plateful of one item. (See page 4 introduction – food and drink).

rambla [<u>ram</u>-bla] – a normally dry river valley. Water may flow seasonally or in wet years. Often used as routes even for vehicles. Vegetation grows up and is periodically washed out.

rey [<u>ray</u>] – king.

reyecillo [ray-e-<u>thee</u>-yo] – a "little" king, young or of small importance.

río [<u>ree</u>-oh] – river.

río <u>culo</u> de <u>per</u>ro. "Dog's arse river" – beautiful valley; shame about the name.

romería [romer –<u>ee</u>-a] – peregrination, usually communal and associated with a *fiesta*.

rosado [roz-are-though] – rose coloured (adj.) a rosé wine (n.)

salchicha [sal-<u>chi</u>-cha] – sausage. Name of the highest point of the Sierra de la Contraviesa, *Cerro de Salchicha* (1,538m).

salchichón [salchi-<u>chon</u>] – a type of sausage (see food glossary page 6)

serrano [serr-<u>an</u>-o] – (adj.) relating to the sierra. (see *jamón*)

sierra [see-<u>air</u>-a] – saw or a range of mountains.

siete [see-<u>ette</u>] – seven.

tabacos [tab-<u>bac</u>-os] – cigarette shop, also the place for postage stamps. See *estanco* which is the same idea.

tajo [<u>ta</u>-ho] – cliff.

tapa [<u>tap</u>-pa] – Lid. Snack (see food and drink page 4).

tostada [tossed-<u>artha</u>] – toasted bread (see food and drink page 4).

tinao [tin-<u>ow</u>] – a covered way, formed when part of a house is built across a street perhaps to join onto the building opposite. One of the distinguishing features of Alpujarran domestic architecture. Reasons are obscure, but the practicalities are that they increase the use of space and help to keep the streets cool.

vereda [verr-<u>ez</u>-tha] – route for the movement of livestock from one area to another. They are marked on topographic maps but usually non-existent on the ground. They remain as rights of way and have a legal width of 20.897m. I thought you would like to know that, not a lot of people do. Another word used for similar routes is cañada, the width of which even less people know.

vieja [vee-<u>e</u>-ha] – old.

vino [vee-<u>no</u>] – wine (see food and drink page 4).

Appendix D – Holiday organisers active in The Alpujarra

Discovery travel

Walking and cycling holidays in the UK and Europe, including a self-led walking tour through The Alpujarra.

Tel: 01904 766564

www.discoverytravel.co.uk/andalucia/

Email: info@discoverytravel.co.uk.

12 Towthorpe Road, Haxby, York YO32 3ND.

Rustic Blue

An English/Spanish run company based in Bubión. They run a fixed centre-guided walking holiday. Also useful to the independent traveller since they operate as a travel and accommodation agency.

Tel: 0034 958 763381

www.rusticblue.com

Barrio La Ermita, 18412, Bubión, Granada, Spain

Andalucian Adventures

Run fixed-centre, hotel-based, guided walking holidays at various locations in Spain, The Alpujarra included. They run painting holidays at the same centres.

Tel: 01453 834137

www.andalucian-adventures.co.uk

Washpool, Horsley, Gloucestershire, GL6 0PP

Sketch and Trek

Holidays for artists who like to walk, with Jeni Rabjohns, the illustrator of this guide.

Email: jrabj@hotmail.com

Useful websites

www.walkalpujarra.co.uk: Guiding service and tailor made holidays by your author.

www.lasalpujarras.com

www.andalucia.co.uk

www.nevadensis.com: Guiding and information service particularly good for adventurous activities and high altitude expeditions.

Appendix E – Altitude Profile Diagrams

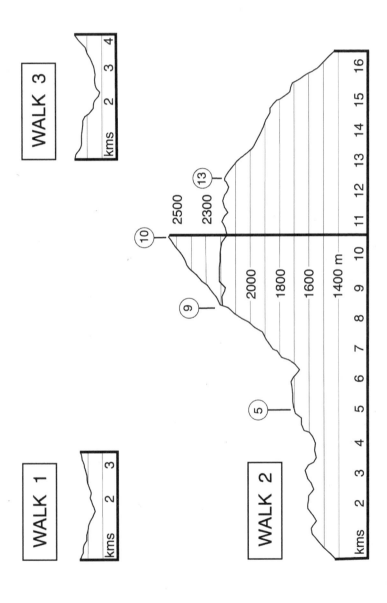

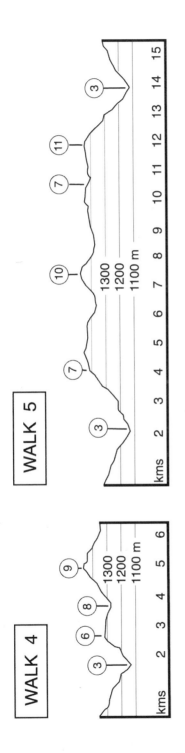

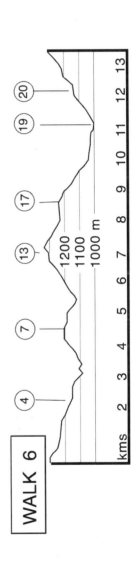

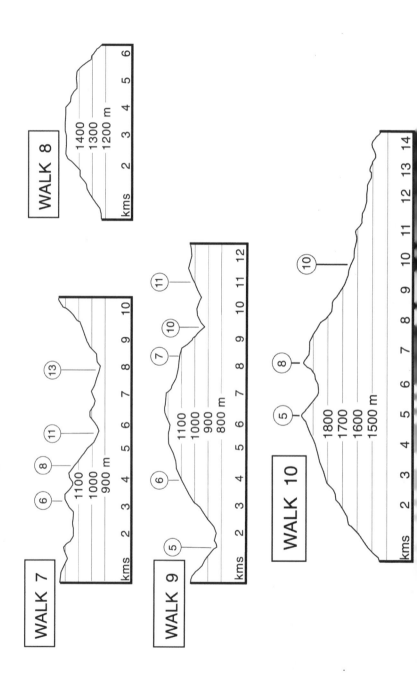

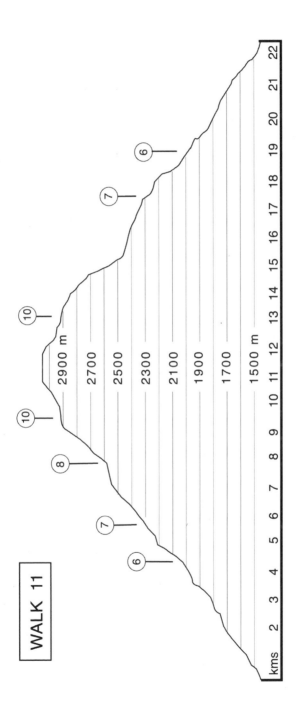

WALK 11

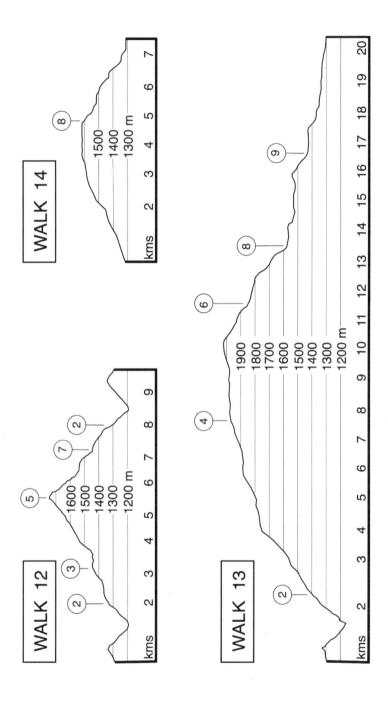

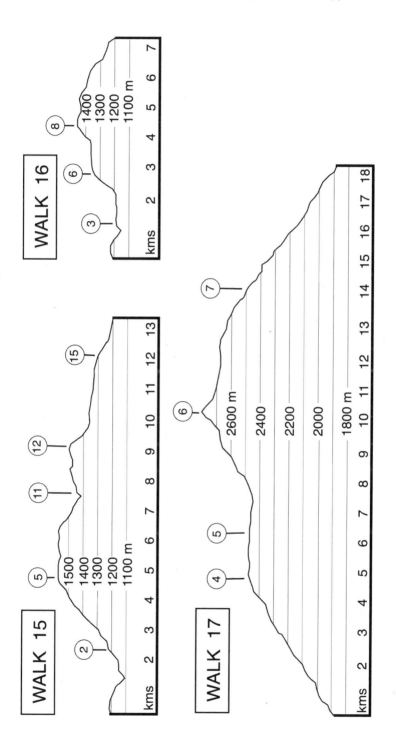

181

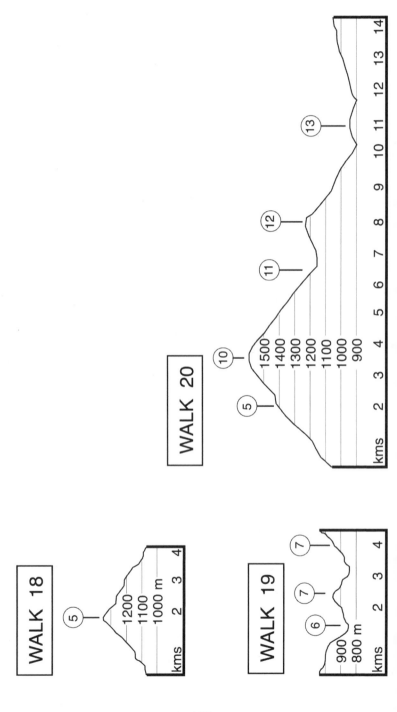

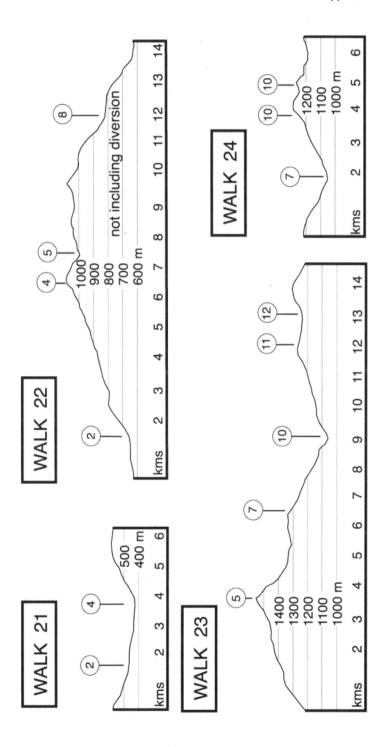

183

Appendix F – Updates and Amendments

Updates

This section includes all of the update information provided on our website up to June 2003, collated into page number order for easy reference. Included here are notes about washed-away bridges, new tracks and other potentially important information. Be sure to read this section before starting any relevant walk and check the website for further updates beyond June 2003.

Page 42

Fact File: La Tahá de Pítres

Buses: They call at Pítres, Pórtugos and Busquístar, see Appendix A. A feeder mini-bus service links Pítres with Mecina at times to connect with the main bus.

Accommodation: Hotels in Pítres, Pórtugos and Mecina. B&Bs in Ferreirola and Busquístar, both being perfect locations for the walker.

Restaurants: In Pítres, Pórtugos, Busquístar, Mecina and Mecinilla. Notable are "El Jardin" (Pítres) for being vegetarian, "Sierra Nevada" (next to the supermarket in Pítres) and "Las Lillas" (low down in Busquístar) for excellent traditional food and ambience. *(June 2003)*

Page 45, point 6 – italic section

All the paragraph –

Busquistar has a splendid position overlooking the gorge, some of the best-maintained terraced land remaining in the area and one of the best-liked eating places and B&B in the Alpujarra.

Page 55, walk 8

Point 1 – Start from the village square of Pítres, walk up between the church and the pharmacy. Fork right 50m after the pharmacy. *(June 2003)*

Page 65, Walk 10

Difficulties: *In addition to the existing paragraph.*

The bridge at point **10** has been washed away. The river is fordable here except in rainy weather or during the late spring thaw. Crossing with dry feet is unlikely at any time. In view of the uncertainty it might be better to do the walk in reverse, thereby giving fewer problems in the event of having to abort.

The absence of the bridge, point **10** is not obvious when walking the reverse route: it is a few metres after a point where an *acequia* temporarily adopts the path as its route and there is a vertical cliff on the the immediate right. A well-used path rises away from the river on the opposite bank. *(Sept 2002)*

Page 65-69, Walk 10: reverse walk notes

The bridge at point **(10)** has been washed away and often the river cannot be forded safely. It is suggested that the walk be done in reverse so that if the circular option has to be aborted, a good there-and-back walk, taking about 4 hours, will be possible

It is a good idea to take sandals so that you can ford the river *and* have dry boots on the other side. You should allow 6 to 8 hours for the circular walk. There is always a lot of water on the paths of this route but it is a 5-star walk: worth getting wet for. The background notes of the original text still apply and are not duplicated here.

1. Start from the main road at the bottom of Trevélez. Using the town plan(page 67) walk uphill to the church in *Plaza Iglesia*. Walk around to the back of the church, passing between it and the bank, and start to go up C.cuesta. On the first bend, 20m after the church take the dirt road to the right, the track heads gently down-hill towards the river bed.

    After about 500m. the track crosses a bco. Once past the *bco.* look out for a path joining it from the left, then 30m later take the path angling up left away from the track. This path branches off the track 50m before some fancy pillars and gate of a house.

    Keep right 100m later at the path junction **(14)**. There are minor turns into fields and to farms but the route always follows the major path, undulating parallel to the west bank of the river and following it upstream. There are usually some wire fence/gates to open/close. It takes about 1hr. to reach **(12)** from **(14)**.

12. Cross the river on the stone-built bridge. The path, now following the east bank often doesn't know if it is a path or a stream, but it is a path. Ignore a rising right branch, just after the bridge.It is about 40mins walk from **(12)** to **(10)**, the missing bridge.

11. The bridge marked on the map here has been washed away. It was only mentioned as a landmark and is of no consequence. 1.5kms afer **(12)** keep left at a clear fork in the path. This point is just where a stone *cortijo* comes into sight on the opposite bank.

10. The path dips a little, begins to coincide with the start of an *acequia* (more paddling) and simultaneously passes a huge boul-der with a near vertical face on the immediate right. This is **(10)** where the bridge used to be, on the opposite bank can be seen some remains of the stonework. 30m. later a branch path forks down to a ford. A clear path can be seen rising from the far bank.

    If the water looks smooth, not white and frothing, and you can see the stony bed, it is probably about calf-deep or less and crossable in safety. **If in doubt, don't**. Taking socks off to keep them dry is a good idea. Keep boots on when crossing

10m. after crossing the river the path bears right and begins a steep zigzag route up the hill at right angles to the river bed, and arrives at **(9)**, a *cortijo*, after about 20 mins.

9. Go left where the path arrives at the front door of the *cortijo*. The path leads, on the contour, through a makeshift fence and into the *bco*. The path leads more or less on the contour, heading for the shoulder of hill. On rounding the shoulder of the hill you are about halfway round the walk, the reward for your efforts being some of the most spectacular views, whichever way you look. There is no shade here but for a good rest, see comments made under (7) of the original text about water, shade and cherry trees. These places are 10 minutes walk away.

   The path begins to follow the top side of a wire fence. 25m later take the left branch of the path as it passes through the fence/gate. The path angles down towards two stone *cortijos* and passes out through the fence again just by the second at **(8)**.

8. The path leads down from the far side of the building, through a very soggy area towards **(7)**, the bridge over the *Río Culo de Perro*.

7. Cross the bridge. **Test the stones for stability before trusting them.** The path angles up from the river in a downstream direction. At a fork, keep left. Pass through a wire fence/gate.

6. Keep left where a path joins from the left. The path zigzags and rounds the shoulder of the hill, the highest point on the walk at about 1950m.

   This high point provides an ideal excuse for sitting and staring. It is about 2 hours walk (5km) from here, back to Trevélez. The path is always obvious and generally descending.

5. A viewpoint on a saddle of hillside. At a ruin about 1km after **(5)** ignore right and left options, keep to the main path which passes just along the lower side of the ruin.

4. Keep left on the main path, ignoring the right turn which has waymarks pointing to *Las Siete Lagunas*.

3. Pass between two buildings immediately on the left and right of the path. During the next 1.5km the path continues to be obvious, passing through two good shady *bcos*. with water running in them. 200m after the second *bco* the path crosses an *acequia* by its mini-bridge. 200m later, take the steeply descending left option. It is 10m after a large white painted *cortijo* on the left, ignore the level path going right.

1. Go right at the first village street. Any downhill option through the village will lead to the mainroad at the bottom of the village **(1)**.

   – *end of Walk 10, reverse walk notes* –

Page 68, Walk 10
Map 10 – The bridge marked as **(11)** no longer exists. It was not used by the route except as a landmark. (see updates for pages 65 and 69) *(Sept 2002)*

Page 69 Walk 10
Point 11 – The bridge marked on the map as a landmark has been washed away (see updates for pages 65 and 68) *(Sept 2002)*

Page 79, Walk 13
Bérchules Village Plan – in the bottom left of the plan, the label **Walk 3** should read **Walk 14** *(Sept 2002)*

Page 80 Walk 12
Point 2 – From the *era* the route turns left and follows a broken wall up, until meeting with a wire mesh fence.

Turn right to keep the mesh fence on the left. Keeping close to the fence the path climbs quite steeply for about 100m. Keep right at a fork in the path (where the left branch passes through the fence). The path begins to diverge from the fence, crosses a level patch of ground heading for a small ruinous *casa de campo* and then onto the stone edged terrace ahead.

Point 3 – Turn right along the track ... *(Sept 2002)*

Page 87, Walk 13
Map 13: About 2km after point 9 there is a new track which cuts and obscures the original path, see update for page 88. *(Sept 2002)*

Page 88, Walk 13
Point 9, – paragraph 3 – The path diverges right to a level slightly higher than the *acequia*. For the next 2km the path follows an undulating course, generally south towards the village. It ignores a right branch into the deep side valley and later there are other minor turns to the right and left to ignore.

About 2km after point 9 there is a new track which cuts and obscures the original path. The path joins it at a hairpin bend: follow the track downhill. Keep right, on the track (ignoring the hairpin left) and look out for the old path which reappears on the right of the track near its end. *(Sept 2002)*

Page 100, Walk 16
Replace all of point 2 as follows:
2. Look for a track on the left, 500m after the supermarket, with a 'stop' sign at its junction with the road. It forks off to the left from a lay-by, passes over a stone built viaduct and continues as a private road leading through some usually locked gates to a house above.

Follow the steep stony path, which branches off the track, before arriving at the viaduct and gates. It climbs very steeply for a few metres then continues up around a small *barranco*, crosses its waters, then passes below the house to rejoin the house driveway just past a second set of lockable gates.

Follow the drive up to the house and turn right, just as the house is reached, to join the path following the *acequia* (3). *(June 2003)*

Page 112, Walk 18

Point 2 – 5 metres past the next bridge, crossing Barranco Zajón, take the path to the left opposite a house. The path winds uphill passing a *casa de campo* on the right, then later makes a zigzag steeply left, ignoring a more level path which continues straight on. A second *casa de campo* is then passed on the left of the path. *(Nov 2002)*

Page 112, Walk 18

Point 3 – second paragraph – Continuing in a generally north-west direction the path comes to a *cortijo*, bends to the left and ... *(Nov 2002)*

Page 116, walk 19

Replace all of point 1:

1. Start at the junction of the main through road where a concrete road zigzags down into the village. Follow the concrete road down, ignoring a small street on the right and arrive in the plaza near Bar La Fuente (2), see village plan (page 113). *(June 2003)*

Page 124, Walk 20

Point 12 – second paragraph – The path soon passes a *casa de campo* and two rectangular *albercas* on the left.

Cross a *barranco* with running water and then another dry *barranco* with a rock spire above the path. At this second *barranco* the path divides and rejoins itself; the upper branch being the true path, the lower an *acequia* which soon rejoins the path. Ignore a right branch which climbs a little to follow a line of poplar trees. At one point the path divides around a wire-fenced olive grove ... *(Sept 2002)*

Page 125, Walk 20

Paragraph 3 – 20m after a zigzag in the track, the path forks left off the track. It passes down through some olive trees to an *era*, crosses the uphill side of it and then drops down to meet the track again. The track leads to a *casa de campo* but the path branches right before the house, downhill, aiming for a copse of poplars in the river bed. Cross on the bridge ... *(Sept 2002)*

Page 134, Walk 22

Point 5 – 200 or 300m later the path curves around to the south. Ignore a minor path on the apex of the bend and after about 50m take a rocky path zigzagging up, right. *(Oct 2002)*

Page 165, Appendix A, Taxis

Órgiva – 958 785589 – Travel agent's office on the street between the petrol station and the traffic lights. *(June 2003)*

Page 166, Appendix A

Route: Granada-Pitres/Bérchules/Alcutar

The list of stops should include Bubión next to Capileira with the same times. *(Sept 2002)*

Page 167, Appendix B, Granada city

Casa del Aljarife: This lodging is no longer recommended. *(June 2003)*

Page 168, Appendix B, La Taha

Mecina: Hotel Alberque de Mecina (**); key symbols, H H Y Y; website www.ocioteca.com/hotelmecina.
Tel: 958 766254; Fax: 958 766255

A happy mixture of spacious rooms, excellent facilities and friendly staff. Pool. English spoken. *(June 2003)*

Page 175, Appendix D, Discovery travel

website: www.discoverytravel.co.uk *(June 2003)*

Errata

These are mostly minor typographical errors and are included here for completeness. The text shown in this section in pale blue is wrong and should be replaced by the text shown in black:

Page 10

Distant sources and ages.
Distinct sources and ages.

Page 20

The ash is scraped to the back and the dough put in to cook.
The hot embers are scraped into the chamber below to help maintain the temperature.

Page 28, point 3 (Italic section)

... path north west ...
... path north east ...

Page 36 line 2

... llama
... lama

Page 46, point 13

... (page 43) ...
... (page 44) ...

Page 48, point 16

... page 55.
... page 56.

Page 48, point 17 (italic section)
... see village plan page 48.
... see village plan opposite.

Page 52, point 13
Map 9 (page 60)...
Map 9 (page 61)...

Page 54, point 16 – italic section paragraph 1
... (see illustrations page 39 and 75)...
... (see illustrations page 40 and 75)...

Page 54, point 16 – italic section, paragraph 2
... , see sketch map page 48
... , see sketch map page 49

Page 78, point 1
... Fuente de las Carmelitas
... Fuente de las Carmelas

Page 81, paragraph 2
... it always had a sherry-ish
... it always has a sherry-ish

Page 81, last paragraph
... (see illustration page 92)
... (see illustration page 93)

Page 96, paragraph 2
Emerging form the scrub, ...
Emerging from the scrub, ...

Page 108, point 4 – paragraph 2
... obvious was out, ...
... obvious way out, ...

Page 124, point 12 – paragraph 2
... rock spine ...
... rock spire ...

Page 125, paragraph 6
... a shrub grown
... a scrub grown

Page 125, point 13 – last line
... barrío ...
... barrio ...

Page 127, paragraph 1 – line 3
... spot for ornithologists and in ...
... spot for ornithologists, ...

Page 134, paragraph 3 – line 3
... tree-filed ...
... tree-filled ...

Pages 138, last paragraph and page 139, first paragraph
... Alcazer ...
... Alcázar ...

Page 150, point 1 – paragraph 2 – line 1
... through there streets ...
... through these streets ...

Page 152, point 4 – line 1
4. Emerge form ...
4. Emerge from ...

Page 152, point 7 – paragraph 2 – line 1
... Monasterío
... Monasterio

Page 156, point 10 – line 1
... Doralhorra
... Daralhorra

Page 157, point 14 – paragraph 4
... c. Cueras
... c. Cuevas

Page 160, point 7 – paragraph 3
... Monasterío
... Monasterio

Page 162, point 5 – paragraph 4
... los Matires.
... los Martires

Page 171, aljibe
... water stone
... water store